TEACHING *Life Lessons*

IN A HOME-CENTERED CHURCH SUPPORTED WAY

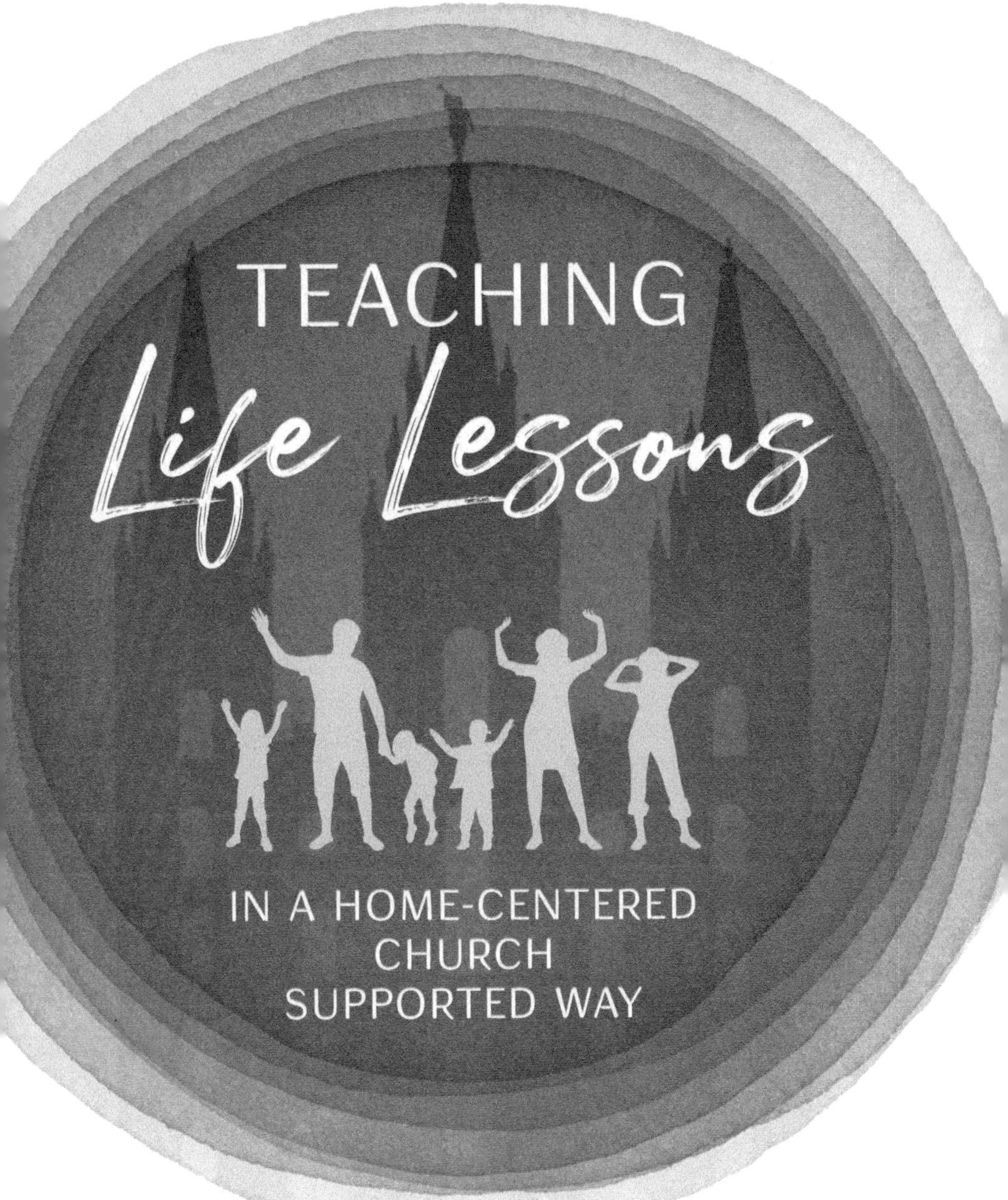

NORMAN C. HILL

CFI
An imprint of Cedar Fort, Inc.
Springville, Utah

Paperback ISBN 13: 978-1-4621-4433-4
Ebook ISBN 13: 978-1-4621-4652-9

Published by CFI, an imprint of Cedar Fort, Inc.
2373 W. 700 S. Suite 100, Springville, UT 84663
Distributed by Cedar Fort, Inc., www.cedarfort.com

Library of Congress Registration Number: 2023942338

Cover design by Shawnda Craig

Edited and typeset by Valene Wood

Printed in the United States of America

10 9 8 7 6 5 4 3 2 1

Printed on acid-free paper

To my children: Ryan, Kristen, Russell, and Kirk

"Lo, children are an heritage of the Lord . . . as arrows are in the hand of a mighty man; so are children . . .

Happy is the man that hath his quiver full of them."

Psalms 127:3–5

Contents

Introduction **1**

Chapter 1: Why Teaching at Home Matters **7**

Chapter 2: How Parents Teach **21**

Chapter 3: When Parents Teach **31**

Chapter 4: Where Parents Teach **41**

Chapter 5: What Parents Teach Best—A Toolbox **51**

- # 1: Developing a Growth Mindset 53
- # 2: Losing Graciously 58
- # 3: Overcoming Grudges 63
- # 4: Getting Organized 69
- # 5: Valuing Money 75
- # 6: Becoming Good Natured 82
- # 7: Looking Out for Others 87
- # 8: Developing Good Manners and Avoiding Rude Behavior 92
- # 9: Developing Empathy 97
- #10: Replacing Envy with Generosity 102
- #11: Living Purposefully 108
- #12: Rolling with the Punches 114
- #13: Doing Your Best 120
- #14: Overcoming Pessimism 126
- #15: Appreciating Gospel Art and Sacred Music 131
- #16: Avoiding Comparisons 138
- #17: Creating a Helping Attitude 143
- #18: Developing Mental Toughness 148
- #19: Deciding You Can't Please Everyone 153

#20: Cultivating Good Friends 159
#21: Learning to Compromise and Adjust 164
#22: Helping Kids Feel Safe in a Tumultuous World 169
#23: Recognizing It's Not All about You 175
#24: Owning Up to Mistakes 180
#25: Fostering Positive Relations with the Opposite Sex 188
#26: Discovering What You Are Good At 196
#27: Making Church a Welcoming Place 204
#28: Teaming Up with Teachers 211
#29: Refrain from Being Quick to Judge 216
#30: Staying Curious 222

Chapter 6: Teaching and Parenting—
Creating Home-Centered Learning Environments 227

About the Author 237

Introduction

Parents are responsible for teaching in the home. We know that. But how? With all of the things which need to be done, how is this very important need met?

And how can parents compete with fast-paced social media or sports, or popular music or movies? How can learning be both instructive and fun rather than getting labeled as "boring"?

President Russell M. Nelson has emphasized that the home should be the "center of gospel learning."[1] The Church's website for Children and Youth encourages the development of life skills not only in teens but also in younger children in a deliberate and conscientious way. It quotes Maryssa Dennis from Church Magazines, saying:

> Identify the life skills that are most important for your children to learn—not only physical skills like preparing food and maintaining a home but also social and emotional skills like interacting with others and handling rejection. Plan activities and service that will allow your kids to practice new skills and contribute positively to the world around them.[2]

Furthermore, as emphasized in *Teaching in the Savior's Way*, this requires parents to plan and structure home-centered activities—not just lessons, but informal learning methods and exercises to develop these life skills:

> But that doesn't mean that good gospel learning happens automatically at home; it takes conscientious effort. . . . You may have a scheduled home evening lesson or family scripture study, but

1. Russell M. Nelson, "Becoming Exemplary Latter-day Saints," *Ensign*, Nov. 2018, 113.
2. Maryssa Dennis, "Teaching Children Essential Life Skills," *Ensign*, Sept. 2020, churchofjesuschrist.org.

> teaching opportunities in the family frequently occur in informal, everyday moments—while eating a meal, doing chores, playing a game, traveling to work or school, reading a book, or watching a movie together. . . . Because such moments are unplanned, you can't prepare for them the way you would prepare for a traditional lesson. . . . Any moment may become a teaching or learning moment.[3]

President Nelson has further suggested that we might need to "transform" or metaphorically "remodel [our] homes" to accomplish the purposes intended by a *home-centered Church-supported* teaching and learning environment.[4]

How can we do that? This book provides both a description of home-centered teaching and learning and specific tools, activities, and methods for teaching and learning in the home. It applies to children of all ages and families of all types.

This is a guidebook that is intended to be used, not simply read. Like any visitor's guidebook, it is linked to a place. In this case, it is tied to home and the lessons that are best learned there: some taught intentionally, others discovered along the way through family activities and interaction. It is about learning by doing.

It's been said that "experience is the best teacher." But sometimes we don't learn from experience. Or we learn the wrong lesson. In fact, two or more family members may even have the same experience and walk away with very different perspectives about what happened. Unless we follow up by discussing experiences together, family members may have very different "learnings" from them. Sharing together what they thought, felt, or learned from an experience or activity not only enriches it but also turns ordinary experiences into powerful "teaching moments."

"Wasn't that great?" one family member may say about an activity or event while another may remark "No, it was the worst." Beyond family members' different attitudes, they may, in fact, have had different "key moments" that determined what they missed or learned.

These differences may occur for a variety of reasons, including the "highs and lows" that may have had during an activity or how an experience ended. Intense "high and lows" or dramatic endings from any experience can overshadow everything else that may have happened. When this occurs,

3. "Suggestions for a Variety of Teaching Settings and Learners," *Teaching in the Savior's Way: For All Who Teach in the Home and in the Church,* churchofjesuschrist.org.

4. Russell M. Nelson, "Becoming Exemplary Latter-day Saints," *Ensign,* Nov. 2018, 113.

family members may "cherry pick" conclusions or even make broad statements that are incomplete or unrepresentative. Here's how this happens:

- *Highs or lows*: That *one aspect* that became a significant emotional event.
- *How it ended*: The last thing that happened that creates a lasting impression.

Highs and lows influence our thinking.

Ordinary or passing moments go unnoticed!

Understanding how we learn from experience can help us discover what, why, and how to have more accurate "learnings." And, importantly as parents, help us plan and design the kind of formal and informal experiences that facilitate learning in all its many forms.

Without "unpacking" the experiences that we have with other family members, we leave it to chance or random developments to decipher what something *meant* and what *generalizations* can be accurately drawn and universally applied. Unpacking or debriefing allows for closer examination of what happened and leads to even more discoveries about ourselves and how things work in the world in which we live.

This book is about purposefully designing learning experiences which build *character, competencies*, and *connections* in families. It is based on gospel principles, and learning design tools and methods that reinforce them.

It aims to do three things:

1. Explain how, when, and where parents can teach formally and informally using *discovery learning* tools.
2. Describe how *discovery learning* works and can be applied in any family setting: single parent, two parent, blended, and grandparent-connected families alike.
3. Provide a practical, hands-on toolkit of *discovery learning activities* which can be used in developing social, emotional, and Christlike attributes.

When the Prophet Joseph Smith was languishing in Liberty Jail and cried out to the Lord for help, he was told that "all these things shall give thee experience, and shall be for thy good" (D&C 122:7). Apparently, what he needed to learn was not self-evident. Through further instruction and discussion with others, he later shared what he learned and what it meant to him.

This discovery learning process of "learning by doing" is emphasized in the introduction to *Come, Follow Me:*

> The aim of all gospel learning and teaching is to deepen our conversion to Heavenly Father and Jesus Christ . . . [W]e're not just looking for new information; we want to become a "new creature" (2 Corinthians 5:17). . . . We should seek after whatever invites the influence of the Spirit and reject whatever drives that influence away.[5]

Come, Follow Me then gives examples on how this can be done. In describing how gospel learning occurs, it stresses using learning methods that allow others to experience gospel principles and then discuss how to apply it. Here's three examples of "learning by doing" emphasized in *Come, Follow Me*:

1. *Participate in object lessons:* "[F]ind ways to let your children participate. They will learn more from an interactive experience than from watching a demonstration."
2. *Role-play.* "When children role-play a situation, they are likely to encounter in real life, they are better able to understand how a gospel principle applies to their lives."[6]
3. *Liken the scriptures to your life*: "[A]sk yourself 'What experiences have I had that are similar to what I am reading?'"[7]

Come, Follow Me is intended as a home-centered resource used by families during the week, supplement by Church-supported lessons on Sundays. As Elder David A. Bednar stressed:

> We should not expect the Church as an organization to teach us or tell us everything we need to know and to do to become devoted disciples and to endure valiantly to the end. Rather, our personal responsibility is to learn what we should learn, to live as we know we should live, and to become who the Master would

5. "Conversion Is Our Goal," *Come, Follow Me—For Individuals and Families,* Old Testament 2022 (The Church of Jesus Christ of Latter-day Saints, 2021).
6. Ibid, "Teaching Young Children,"
7. Ibid, "Ideas to Improve Your Personal Scripture Study."

> have us become. And our homes are the ultimate setting for learning, living, and becoming.[8]

None of us are naturally skilled at everything. We need to learn life skills; we are not born with them. Skills and talents come from discovery, practice, and often some failures. It is in trying that we succeed.

8. David A. Bednar, "Prepared to Obtain Every Needful Things," *Ensign*, May 2019, 102.

Chapter 1

Why Teaching at Home Matters

"Everybody knows how to raise children," the humorist P. J. O'Rourke once said, "except the people who have them." It's often easier to see what other people's children need than our own children. It's even easier to see and harder to do anything about our grandchildren. Most unsolicited suggestions by grandparents are as unwanted and as they are unheeded.

So, what are parents (and maybe even grandparents) supposed to do? It can be tricky. But with patience and an openness to new ideas, it's possible to raise responsible children and teach them those life lessons that can only be learned at home.

There is an old saying that if the student hasn't learned, then the teacher hasn't taught. While this may unnecessarily put all of the burden on the teacher, at least it provides an easy way for parents to figure out if their children are learning the life lessons needed to survive in this world and spiritually qualify to progress in the next one. When those life lessons don't seem to be part of children's daily life—from preschoolers to teens—then it is an invitation for parents to act differently and teach persuasively.

It is not enough for parents to simply proclaim the gospel to their children; they must persist until important messages are understood and incorporated by them. As the Doctrine and Covenants emphasizes:

> Inasmuch as parents have children in Zion . . . that teach them not to understand the doctrine of repentance, faith in Christ the Son of the living God, and of baptism and the gift of the Holy Ghost by the laying on of hands, when eight years old, the sin be on the heads of the parents. (D&C 68:25)

President Russell M. Nelson has stressed this responsibility even more emphatically:

> That commandment places responsibility and accountability for the teaching of children squarely upon the shoulders of the parents. The proclamation to the world regarding the family warns that individuals "who fail to fulfill family responsibilities will one day stand accountable before God."[1]

In many ways, the Book of Mormon is a useful "lesson manual" in teaching children regardless of their age because this family saga shows how, where, and what life lessons parents can best teach and the consequences that can occur when not done sufficiently. It even begins with "I, Nephi, having been born of goodly parents . . ." and goes from there to talk about the trials and triumphs of extended family relations for a thousand years. There is much to be learned directly and indirectly about home-centered, church-supported teaching from its pages.

It is with some trepidation that anyone writes about how and what parents can best teach at home. I am no exception. I'm neither a perfect parent nor a transcendent teacher. Instead, I'm doing my best both learning from my (now) adult children and trying to avoid making too many mistakes along the way. My wife Raelene and I have been blessed with four children and 16 grandchildren. After she passed away in 2015, I married Stephanie in 2017 who also has four children with an additional 21 grandchildren. Our *bonus family* of eight children and 37 grandchildren is, if it is anything, quite an adventure. I hope to share what we and others have learned about home-centered teaching as we live, laugh, and love together.

DISCOVERY LEARNING

Traditional ways of teaching through lectures or even reading and discussion have limited use these days as electronic media and methods are increasingly replacing traditional methods. What parents haven't heard the familiar refrain from their children when having a family discussion: "This is boring." And even if you haven't heard it that doesn't mean it wasn't thought about! It's hard to compete with computer graphics and mesmerizing animation.

There is, however, an alternative to traditional methods that is effective and entertaining. Like any skill, it takes a little practice to learn, but once mastered can easily be used in a variety of different settings. Instead of

1. Russell M. Nelson, "Set in Order Thy House," *Ensign*, Nov. 2001, 70.

just telling or even discussing gospel principles, let family members experience them together and enhance their own understanding and judgment by applying them in their daily lives. This "flips the narrative" by changing parents from mere learning enforcers to *designers, facilitators, guides, and leaders.*

It's often said that "experience is the best teacher." It's never been truer than today. In fact, it may be the only truly effective method available to help children learn the enduring life lessons that will enable them to grow socially and spiritually living "in the world" without becoming "of the world." It can be challenging to find or create the right experiences that develop fundamental life habits, but it is possible.

"Discovery learning" or learning by doing is how parents at home (and teachers at church) can teach children without resorting to lecturing, browbeating, or nagging. It involves a fundamental shift from how parents often think about their role and what methods they use to teach their children. Discovery learning is an active, participatory approach that is more about helping children learn life lessons for themselves than simply imparting information to them hoping that they will retain it. In fact, discovery learning is the single most effective way to enhance moral agency by changing attitudes, developing skills, and modifying behaviors in developing Christlike attributes.

As a parent, grandparent, and church leader; I found that children and others typically want to "do things for themselves." They don't want to be told what to do and often resist it—even when it seems like giving them "the answer" would simply be the most efficient way to go. It isn't. It never was. In fact, one time when my oldest son was a teenager, I overheard him say to a friend at church, "I ought to number my dad's lectures. He says the same thing so often I could just call out a number and save us both some time."

I was shocked. I didn't realize my advice to him was having so little impact. It certainly wasn't my intention to be dismissed, but that is what was occurring. Since then, I've tried to use a different approach by asking myself, "What do my children need to learn?" and then, "How can I create situations where that is most likely to happen?"

Whenever a learner accepts an invitation to act, it is, according to Elder Richard G. Scott, "an exercise in agency that permits the Holy Ghost to communicate a personalized message suited to their individual needs." Elder Scott then explained, "Creating an atmosphere of participation enhances the probability that the Spirit will teach more important lessons than you can communicate."[2]

Effective teachers create many different opportunities for learners to use their agency through open-ended case studies, real-life stories, gospel-themed games, and problematic situations that require problem-solving and decision-making. This can change the entire learning experience and outcome in both the classroom and in the home. Instead of a home or class of students, there is instead a cluster of learners, and all are teachers.

My friend Bill Dyer, former Dean of the Marriott School of Business at BYU, wrote a book years ago called *Insight to Impact*. In it, he describes the fundamental difference between our *intentions*—what we hope to achieve—and the *impact* which others may instead experience—what actually happens. There is often a large gap between the two, he notes, so it is vitally important to constantly ask:

> Is what I intended to occur having the desired impact on others?[3]

For instance, when I intend to give helpful advice is it interpreted instead as criticism? When I intend to point out ways to improve, is it viewed as telling someone they are not good enough? When I intend to praise or recognize positive effort, is it viewed as superfluous cheerleading?

The best way to determine if our intentions are having the desired impact is to observe the results. For example, are "teaching moments" dreaded or welcomed? When we discuss as a family being more kind to each other, are there fewer fights and disagreements? When we talk about forgiveness, are old grudges laid to rest?

Assessing our impact—and determining if it matches our intentions—requires keen observational skills. Without them, discovery learning methods are incomplete.

DEVELOPING OBSERVATIONAL SKILLS

The prophet Mormon was selected by Ammaron to receive the plates of his people—and eventually abridge them as the Book of Mormon—because he was "quick to observe" (Mormon 1:2). Mormon even says that the record he makes comes from "the things which I have both seen and heard" (Mormon

2. Richard G. Scott, "To Learn and to Teach More Effectively," Brigham Young University Campus Education Week, 21 Aug. 2007, speeches.byu.edu.
3. William G. Dyer, *Insight to Impact: Strategies for Interpersonal and Organizational Change* (Brigham Young University Press, 1976).

1:1). In other words, firsthand observations. Developing good observational skills is essential in discovery teaching and learning.

Discovery learning relies on five different methods for home-centered teaching: structured experiences, role plays, case studies, simulations, and games. They stress acting or doing and then reflecting or debriefing, generalizing, and applying what was learned. They aim to let participants experience something—an activity or event—then reflect on what happened, what seemed to work and not work, and how certain "learnings" can then be applied in other real-life settings.

In creating, adapting, applying, and facilitating such discovery learning activities, parents and teachers need a way of seeing and thinking about them so that results from planned activities get translated into character-building attitudes and skills. It can be easy to draw the wrong conclusion from various activities ("my brother's never helpful") or only see the activity as a game with no real-life application ("I'm not really that way with others, just here"). Guided discussion after any discovery activity is essential to consider options and decide on ways to act in daily life.

Almost any activity—planned or unplanned—can be used as the "doing" part of discovery learning. The two key components of this "activity stage" are participating and observing.

There can be a lot of excitement and fun in any discovery learning activity but, unless some facilitated discussion occurs afterward, there will be little actual learning. Or worse. Due to inexperience or a single incident, family members may actually draw inaccurate conclusions based on a one-time experience.

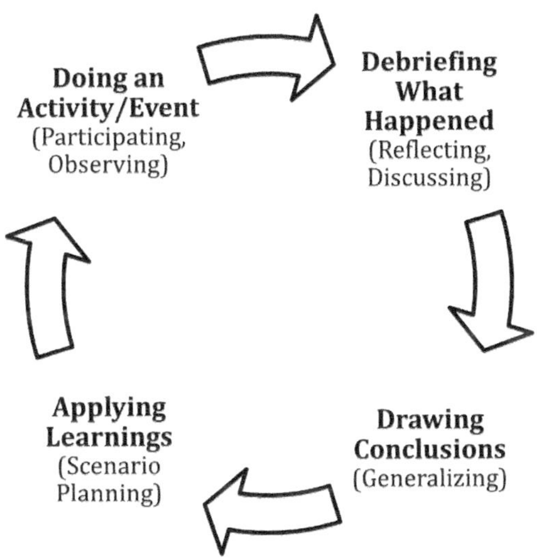

We draw erroneous conclusions all the time. We backtrack from what happened and assign motives to other family members that may not be what they intended at all.

"She's mad because I won." "He's pouting because he didn't get what he wanted."

"She did that just to sabotage me."

It can be challenging to resist the natural temptation to jump to a quick conclusion and instead slow down and discuss what may have actually happened and how our observations and interpretations match up with others. Recognizing our interpretations can either be spot on or way off is a fundamental aspect of discovery learning. We can "overthink" things disconnected from what was either intended or what may have occurred. Or we can fail to notice something when we are distracted or caught up in a game or activity.

REALIZATION AND TRANSFORMATIONAL QUESTIONS

The purpose of the gospel is to bring us to Christ. The programs of the Church and the various ways that we teach each other are all intended to help achieve that divine purpose.

The Savior taught by using questions that both provoked a re-examination among His listeners as well as a call to action. In some cases, He asked questions to help listeners *realize* how they could *think* about situations differently. At other times, He asked questions for them to *picture* how they could *act* differently.

Both are important. Realization is something of an awakening by a person to new possibilities, seeing themselves and others in a new light. While transformation is helping someone enhance their ability, actions, or understanding. They work together to change how we see the world, our place in it, and how we go about bringing ourselves and our neighbors closer to our Heavenly Father.

Here are some questions the New Testament records the Savior asking others to help His listeners think differently, to come to a different realization about themselves, and see their place in the world differently:

REALIZATION

- "But whom say ye that I am?" (Matthew 16:15)
- "The baptism of John, whence was it? from heaven, or of men?" (Matthew 21:25)
- "Why tempt ye me, ye hypocrites? . . . Whose is this image and superscription?" (Mathew 22:18, 20)
- "Why reason ye, because ye have no bread? perceive ye not yet, neither understand? have ye your hearts yet hardened? Having eyes,

see ye not? and having ears, hear ye not? and do ye not remember?" (Mark 8:17–18)

- "Who touched me?" (Mark 5:33)

These questions help us change our point of view, our mindset, and see the world differently. The Savior also asked questions to help us change the way that we act and our reasons and motives behind those actions, to act out of love and in faith.

Transformation

- "Wilt thou be made whole?" (John 5:6)
- "Why are ye fearful, O ye of little faith?" (Matthew 8:26)
- "Wherefore didst thou doubt?" (Matthew 14:31)
- "Then said Jesus unto the twelve, Will ye also go away?" (John 6:67)
- "What is written in the law? how readest thou?" (Luke 10:26)
- "Simon, son of Jonas, lovest thou me more than these?" (John 21:15)

As we strive to submit our will to God's—to think and act more like Him—we change our character, we are no longer the same person, we are, as the apostle Peter said, "partakers of the divine nature" (2 Peter 1:4). The questions that we ask ourselves and others can help us achieve that ultimate goal.

The activity book the Church distributed some years ago gave examples of games or activities for Church groups and families that could be played outdoors including discussion questions to assist in debriefing what happened and what could be learned from such activities about physical, social, intellectual, and spiritual abilities. Many of these were revised and others added when the Church created the Children and Youth website (https://www.churchofjesuschrist.org/youth/childrenandyouth/youth).

In discovery learning, debriefing can occur either with all family members or one-to-one with individual family members. It can be used following a planned or unplanned activity. It involves getting everyone to process or discuss what really happened and what actions led to others' reactions.

The best way to debrief an event or activity is to stick to asking *what* and *how* questions and avoid getting into *why* things may have happened in a certain way. Jumping to conclusions too soon often leads to inaccurate perspectives. Assigning motives to others is never a good idea, either. It leads to backbiting and gossip.

So, don't allow "incriminating questions" among family members when debriefing such as:

"Why did you do that?"
"Why didn't you help me?"
"Why are you always against me?"

So, instead help family members look at *actions* and *reactions by* using questions "what" and "how" like these:

"*What* happened when Josh grabbed the ball?"
"*How* did you feel when Judy put her arm around you and brought you back into the circle?"
"*What* did Alyssa do when Scott yelled at Jesse?"

Rather than drawing conclusions at this stage, debriefing focuses on being very clear about actions and reactions so that everyone looks at an activity in the same way. If possible, try to encourage family members to identify as many "if/then" situations and outcomes as possible. In other words, "if this happens, then what is the likely outcome?"

A good way to begin is by asking the question:

What surprised you about someone's reaction during this activity?

After asking this question, it's then possible to dig a little deeper together about each surprise or unexpected response. A good follow up question might be:

If that surprised you, then what does it say about the way people can react in such situations?

In today's world, there is a heavy focus on individual satisfaction and personal fulfillment. Sometimes it is difficult to see things as others see them, to have the kind of God-like empathy that Enoch witnessed as he saw the "heavens weep."

> And it came to pass that the God of heaven looked upon the residue of the people, and he wept; and Enoch bore record of it, saying: How is it that the heavens weep, and shed forth their tears as the rain upon the mountains?
>
> And Enoch said unto the Lord: How is it thou canst weep, seeing thou are holy, and from all eternity to all eternity? (Moses 7:28–29)

Empathy is an essential God-like characteristic that allows us not only to understand the world better but also to make our own sphere of influence better. It's how family members really help each other, teach each other, and support each other. Not by lecturing or telling them what they "should" do, but by digging into what happened in various situations and recognizing what actions lead to positive or negative reactions. By unpacking events or activities in this way, debriefing leads to better generalizations about everyday events, Christ-like attributes, and gospel living.

A valid generalization is a broad statement about common reactions and their impact on others. They are supported by observation, facts, and discussion. For instance, "wickedness never was happiness" is a well-known generalization about gospel living from the scriptures.

Discovery learning can help us make valid generalizations from either structured activities or life experiences. Rather than relying only on authority figures, we can learn from our own experience to choose good over evil—which is exactly what the Lord told Adam and Eve in the Garden of Eden is our primary purpose on earth.

Deeper understanding and better generalizations come from close observation coupled with confirmation from others. Who better than other family members are as interested and committed to helping us test and assess what we conclude from an experience? They are in the best position to give ongoing support in a safe and loving way. They can also help us avoid jumping too quickly to conclusions without considering alternatives.

Asking ourselves, "What other ways could this situation be viewed?" helps us slow down and draw better conclusions. For instance, when Captain Moroni wrote to Pahoran asking for more support for his army, he erroneously accused him of neglect and sitting "upon your throne in a state of thoughtless stupor" (Alma 60:7). As it turns out, Captain Moroni jumped to a wrong conclusion. Paharon was doing his best to fight off dissenters himself, which he told Captain Moroni about in a subsequent letter.

Some ways to avoid jumping too quickly to conclusions and instead drawing better conclusions based on observation and collaboration is by asking questions like the following:

- What would Jesus do?
- How might someone very different than me view this situation?
- How can I check if what seems to me to be occurring, is what seems to be occurring for others?
- Am I assuming "good intent" by others or assuming the worst?
- Is there a similar situation from the scriptures that I can use as a guide?

Drawing valid conclusions helps us make better choices in daily living and enables us to apply gospel principles in our everyday lives. It's not enough to know how to live the gospel, it is also necessary for us to apply what we know. This *transference* is what all gospel teaching aims to achieve.

Transfer of learning occurs when family members recognize how methods for handling various situations at home can lead to better results outside the home as well. It's about "connecting the dots" everywhere and all of the time by using the discovery learning cycle and its methods in everyday living.

The last step in the discovery learning cycle is to apply "learnings" in everyday life. Without applying newfound insights or skills, family members may have had a great experience, but they've missed the benefit of getting better together. Some ways to invite family members to act in better ways are to consider some questions like these:

- What do you know now that you didn't know before?
- Now what? What does this mean for our family?
- How can we help each other remember what we've learned without nagging?

If families make the discovery learning process a habit, then they will have more shared experiences together that allow personal growth and development. It is a very active coaching role for parents who will find there is less lecturing and more sharing insights together. Teachers at Church can apply the same methods and expect to get similar results. Instead of standard lectures or routine class discussions with obvious answers to leading or rhetorical questions, discovery learning promotes moral agency and deep learning. In fact, children in the family or students in a class can become the "teachers" by planning and leading their own discovery learning activities by creating experiences together or posing problems that family members address together.

This transformational learning and teaching process focuses on conversion to gospel principles, not merely classroom compliance. It can be intimidating at first because there is less overt control by the teacher or parent and more unpredictability about the outcomes from an activity. But with a few tips and a little practice, this shift towards a more effective teaching and learning method will become second nature. It is teaching in the Savior's way by using real life experiences to live and love as He did.

GETTING STARTED TOGETHER

So, let's get started. Teaching and learning together in a home-centered, church-supported way starts with *joining up*. We choose to enlist, to get started, to go together. Like early pioneer scouting expeditions, the terrain can be uncertain and maybe a little or a lot different than expected. Yet, despite having a general idea of the needed direction, it still takes common consent to make regular progress each day. Even wagon trains rely on shared agreement, not merely giving and receiving orders as many pioneer histories and records show.

John the Revelator offered a similar perspective when he told us the Savior waits to be invited in and never forces Himself to be heard.

> Behold, I stand at the door, and knock; if any man will hear my voice, and open the door, I will come in to him, and will sup with him, and he with me. (Revelation 3:20)

THE CHALLENGE TO BECOME

Elder Dallin H. Oaks, First Counselor in the First Presidency, has said that our ultimate goal is "far more than acquiring knowledge. It is not enough for us to be *convinced* of the gospel; we must act and think so that we are *converted* by it. In contrast to the institutions of the world, which teach us to *know* something, the gospel of Jesus Christ challenges us to *become* something."[4]

When we gather together in the restored gospel, we have a chance to process, decode, analyze, and apply gospel principles. Like amphibians, we live in two different worlds and must learn to navigate each of them effectively. Amphibians come by such things as gills and webbed feet naturally to help them survive either on land or in the water. We must acquire the dexterity to live in the world but not become overwhelmed by it through trial and error, experience and observation, study and prayer.

UNLEARNING

Learning requires judgment without becoming judgmental, not simply of others but also of ideas, practices, and aspirations. As we gain new knowledge and insights, we may need to sicard some things we've "learned" in the past. The new *For the Strength of Youth Guide* emphasizes that "Heavenly Father wants His daughters and sons to always be learning. . . . Look for opportunities to expand your mind and your skills. These opportunities can include formal education at school or vocational training as well as informal learning from sources you trust. . . . The more you learn, the more you can build God's kingdom and influence the world for good."[5]

Learning involves acquiring new knowledge and skills as well as new insights about the world around us. It can also require re-examining old

4. Dallin H. Oaks, "The Challenge to Become," *Ensign,* Nov. 2000, 32.
5. "Ttuth will make you free," *For the Strength of Youth: A Guide for Making Choices* (The Church of Jesus Christ of Latter-day Saints, 2022), churchofjesuschrist.org.

habits or beliefs. Learning is being open-minded enough to recognize that as we grow some things we've learned in the past may need to be discarded. For instance, we know that we are divine daughters and sons of Eternal Parents with our own eternal possibilities. Anything which limits or contradicts this divine perspective about us or others is inconsistent with this eternal truth.

In the well-known song "You've Got to be Carefully Taught" from the Broadway play South Pacific, the lyrics include these lines:

> You've got to be taught to be afraid
> Of people whose eyes are oddly made,
> And people whose skin is a different shade—
> You've got to be carefully taught.
>
> You've got to be taught before it's too late,
> Before you are six or seven or eight
> To hate all the people your relatives hate—
> You've got to be carefully taught![6]

Unlearning can be difficult and awkward at any age. Galileo found it so difficult for people to unlearn that even after he demonstrated that the sun did not revolve around the earth, many did not accept it. Columbus, too, had many doubters who would not unlearn that the earth was flat. Even today there is a serious "flat earth society" that is gaining popularity around the globe. And, of course, the Prophet Joseph Smith had many who would not unlearn what they had been taught and were unwilling to accept that the heavens, in fact, are still open and the Bible does not contain the last and final revelation from God.

An acquaintance likes to say that unlearning is like pouring water out of a glass and replacing it with something else—say, a smoothie or a milkshake, for example. While perhaps it is a helpful example, it skims over the difficulty that is often involved in replacing something we *know* with something brand new to us. Missionaries often see investigators struggle with new concepts and strive to bring them closer to true doctrine so the Holy Ghost can testify to them. Yet, laden with their own accumulated truisms and artifacts from their everyday life, letting go can be hard to do.

Learning at any age broadens our perspective, introduces us to new ways of experiencing the world, and helps us acquire new abilities as well as tools to see things the way the Savior sees them, experience things the way

6. Richard Rodgers & Oscar Hammerstein II, "You've Got to Be Carefully Taught," *South Pacific* (Williamson Music Company, 1949).

He experiences them, know things the way He knows them. Like learning a foreign language and living in an unfamiliar place, if we are to be more than tourists in the Kingdom of God, then we must both learn the culture and customs of the place He invites us to call home and successfully share that invitation with others.

IMMERSIVE STUDY

Reading the scriptures introduces us to the "vocabulary" of this new language of God-like living but, as anyone who has tried to learn a language knows, what is spoken on the street can be very different from what is included in a textbook. Studying the grammar is essential in learning a new language (what is sometimes referred to as "*knowing that*") but interacting with others is actually required to communicate (what is often called "*knowing how*").

Dil Parkinson, a BYU linguistic professor, noted in a devotional address that direct teaching can be structured, but the kind of real learning that is required to speak a new language comes mostly from indirect experience. This realization often dawns on students slowly, and at first it can even anger them. It is much harder to teach and learn a language indirectly through experience than directly through vocabulary cards and repetitively conjugating verbs in the proper tense. Direct teaching is necessary to get started but it must largely give way to indirect learning to acquire fluency in a new language.[7]

Indirect learning does not always have an immediate payoff. But those who throw themselves into many different activities, working around and through their frustration until a breakthrough finally comes, eventually win the day. They know it when it occurs. The difference is astonishing.

There is a kind of mystery involved here in moving from a theoretical knowledge to a practical one, figuring out how to develop those habits of tongue, mind, and heart that allow us to function as native speakers. It is hard to describe but easy to notice when it happens.

Gospel learning may similarly be a dual process of directly gaining important information—what is sometimes called additive knowledge—about the scriptures, Church history, and General Conference messages—while immersive study enables the Holy Ghost to testify of divine truths which enhance our divine nature.

7. Dilworth B. Parkinson, "We Have Received, and We Need No More," Brigham Young University devotional, 2 Mar. 2004, speeches.byu.edu.

SUMMARY

While I was serving as a mission president, Elder David A. Bednar visited our mission and was asked during several zone meetings about teaching methods. He often emphasized the importance of *showing* more than *telling* and then urged missionaries to "get out of the way and let the Holy Ghost do the rest." For good reason, the scriptures say that if we don't have the Spirit, we shouldn't teach. Discovery learning relies on showing and then relying on the Holy Ghost for guidance in observing, generalizing, and applying gospel principles to everyday life.

Chapter 2

How Parents Teach

In the October 2018 General Conference, President Russell M. Nelson announced a new focus on home-centered, church-supported teaching. "As Latter-day Saints, we have become accustomed to thinking of 'church' as something that happens in our meetinghouses, supported by what happens at home," he said. "We need an adjustment to this pattern. It is time for a *home-centered Church*, supported by what takes place inside our branch, ward, and stake buildings."[1] As a result, an integrated *Come, Follow Me* curriculum was also announced with an emphasis on regular study and discussion in the home using a standardized curriculum supplemented by Sunday instruction.

This changes everything! Flipping the narrative from "What did you learn at church this week?" to "What did you learn at home this week?" While still in transition, many teachers and parents are experimenting with this new focus on *how* and *where* we learn gospel principles so that we can apply them in our daily lives. When it comes to personal change and development, parents, teachers, and researchers have long recognized that what happens in the home is far more important than what happens at church or even at school. The home is the truest and best learning lab—not just for children and teens, but for adults as well.

But simply *declaring* it doesn't make it so. It is one thing to *talk* about home-centered, church-supported teaching, it is quite another thing to *make it happen*—both at home and at church. Like anything else, learning

1. Russell M. Nelson, "Opening Remarks," *Ensign*, Nov. 2018, 6.

how to make home-centered, church-supported teaching really work takes focus and discipline and concerted effort.

Teaching at home is not the same as teaching at church. Home is more informal, less structured, more intimate. And, unlike teachers at school or church, parents may not be given the same credit for "knowing" about some topics as formal teachers. It's called "social distance"; and while there are many advantages of parents teaching at home, there are a few disadvantages which parents must recognize and address. For instance, they are not able to engage and disengage in the same way as formally assigned teachers, whether these are teachers of church, school, piano, or other form of learning. Unlike others, parents are always there, always around, always "on duty."

Like gospel learning itself, home-centered gospel teaching methods also require preparation, study, and conscious effort to improve. And there is no graduation day, no finish line.

The home, then, is a place not just for conveying information but most importantly for processing and dealing with life events. In fact, it is this home-based *context* that makes gospel principles relevant as well as memorable, germane as well as pragmatic, and habitual as well as complete.

Getting the desired results from home-centered, church-supported teaching requires a shift in our *mindset* as well as in our *delivery methods.* What we teach—the doctrine of Christ—and how we teach it—both at home and at church—change dramatically when we consistently keep in mind our *purpose* is *conversion* and our *goal* is to *bring others to Christ* whether they are family members at home or learners at church.

HOW WE LEARN AT HOME

Whether at home or church, we learn both *formally* and *informally.* Formal learning typically includes a "lesson" with structured objectives and a formal lesson plan. Informal learning is more emergent and generally occurs while debriefing life experiences together. Each has its uses, benefits, and place.

Prior to the internet and electronic devices, it was fairly easy to identify when formal learning occurred and when it did not. Today, the lines are blurred between formal and informal learning, and they often occur simultaneously. For instance, we might take a formal class on Family History or Self-Reliance in order to acquire a new set of skills or expand our knowledge base. This more formal instruction can bleed over to informal, self-directed learning on the internet by learning related skills or becoming immersed in more specialized topics.

Learning and teaching at home occurs just as interactively with both formal and informal learning. Children typically "watch and learn" not only from their parents but also from siblings, neighbors, TV, and social media influencers as well. A 30-minute family discussion once a week is not likely to be more influential in either children or adults' lives than the barrage of other more entertaining electronic or print-related media. It takes more.

What's a person to do? Take away all electronics, keep kids at home, and live in a cave? Protecting ourselves and our children is certainly important. There are plenty of negative influences in the world. And taking a stand and taking control is what parenting and Christ-like living are all about. But "how" and "when" we intervene, teach, listen, mentor, counsel, and share make all the difference between having the desired impact we want on family members or being ignored.

Years ago, when Bill Dyer was then dean of the business school at BYU, I helped with some research he was doing for his book *Creating Closer Families: Principles of Positive Family Interaction.* Researching a wide variety of families in the Church where two-way communication predominated and gospel principles were inoculated, we made a surprising discovery. These families, rather than having strict adherence to daily scripture study and weekly Family Home Evening, instead were somewhat uneven in how often they held family meetings and had family scripture study. But they kept trying and didn't get discouraged when they faltered. They kept at it. Nor did they have a lot of family rules posted on a bulletin board, but instead had just a few of them. But they fiercely held each other—parents as well as children—to those standards. There were some things they were unwilling to compromise.

OPEN HEART DISCUSSIONS

These "unwritten family rules" varied across the families we studied. For some, doing well in school mattered a lot. For others, sports or extracurricular activities were encouraged. In still others, household chores were broadly distributed and jobs outside the home mandated at a young age. Despite these many variations, these families had certain expectations about themselves and how they related to others, which they talked about often.

Known as "open heart discussions," they defined the type of intentional parenting that creates closer families. These discussions may not have happened often, but when a significant event, moment, or circumstance created it, they gathered together as a family and discussed what was happening and its implications.

As the name suggests, *open heart discussions* are meaningful conversations that focus on personal and family virtues: Christ-like virtues. Some of these virtues are in the Thirteenth Article of Faith—being honest, true, chaste, benevolent, virtuous, and doing good to all men—while other important principles and practices are described elsewhere in the scriptures and extolled in general conference.

Open heart discussions can take many different forms: spontaneous or planned, more formal "teaching moments" or more informal comments or questions. They can be daily downloads or occasional activity debriefs. They send a clear message to children about what matters and why. These "deep dives" when the timing is right are as much about connecting and bonding as they are about the words exchanged.

There is an old saying that "when the student is ready, the teacher will appear." Timing is everything. There are times when we are all tired or worn out or just plain need a little time to ourselves. Don't intrude on either your children's or your spouse's necessary "alone time." But there are also limits. It may be difficult to discern "excuses" from "reasons" when figuring out readiness but recognizing the differences for each family member matters.

ESSENTIAL QUESTIONS

Families thrive on traditions, routines, and rituals. These all provide opportunities for daily discussions. Simply by revising some of the ways we may typically ask each other about our day, we can have more meaningful family discussions. Rather than simply asking "How did your day go?" Here's some questions that bring out thoughts, feelings, and experiences for a "deeper dive" and more interactive discussions with other family members:

- Did you get a chance to help anyone today?
- What's something that happened that you feel good about?
- What was the hardest part of your day?
- What's something nice that you did for someone today? What's something nice someone did for you?
- What was something you learned today (not in class)?

These discussion starters may not produce "thunder and lightning" each time you ask them, but the more habitual you are in asking and listening, the more likely they will become part of your family culture.

It's often noted that "children learn by example" which means that parents (as well as other siblings) are important role models. But beyond this observation, here are the ways that parents teach family members in the home:

- Via formal and informal instruction: lessons and discussions
- Through shared experiences: doing things together
- When telling and retelling family stories
- By the Spirit, who teaches us "all things" (John 14:26)
- Through service, which broadens our point of view
- With reinforcement during Church classes and meetings

FORMAL AND INFORMAL FAMILY INSTRUCTION

We learn through prepared lessons and presentations as well as through spontaneous and unplanned events. A birth, a funeral, an accident can affect us as much as any well-designed lesson. How family members respond to unusual situations can have a lasting impact.

A traditional view of learning at home is that children learn what they are formally taught. While it's clear that occurs, even more learning occurs from ordinary, daily interactions and activities. This kind of learning has been equated with a kind of *family apprenticeship* resulting from informal *guided participation.*

This type of family apprenticeship is what researchers have found most significant in homeschooling that can be applied to overall childhood development. In his book *Educating Children at Home,* British researcher Dr. Alan Thomas notes the advantage of homeschooling is the availability of regular inquiry and discussion between children and parent/teachers:

> What struck me most of all . . . was the constant opportunity for informal learning, especially through social, often incidental conversation. Whether they were out walking, sitting around the kitchen table, engaged in some other activity such as drawing, making something, working on a project, eating, out in the car, or even reading, there was an incredible amount of spontaneous incidental talk.[2]

This customized, individualized learning begins with a "lesson" but then continues throughout the day and can even spill over throughout the week based on a child's interests. Researchers found that what children learned during these spontaneous discussions remained with them much

2. Alan Thomas, *Educating Children at Home* (Bloomsbury Publishing, 1998), 4.

longer and could be repeated or explained better than when formally taught in a regular classroom.

SHARED EXPERIENCES

Teachers have the advantage of "social distance" over parents who have a much more comprehensive role. Teachers do not share the same family dynamics as parents and siblings. For instance, a neighbor may be able to help your children learn to ride a bike easier than you as a parent because their tips and advice are more readily accepted as suggestions than yours which may be interpreted only as criticism. Teenagers, especially, may see parents' suggestions as personal slights. Teens may see their parents as overly anxious about drugs, crime, success, and other expectations to the point where they may find it difficult to have meaningful conversations without feeling judged.

"There's just so much more emotional weight that goes into teaching your own kids," says Dr. Vasco Lopes, school psychologist and Columbia University professor.[3] This unique aspect is an important characteristic of teaching at home. Family members never really ignore their relationships with each other even when discussing gospel principles. They are intertwined.

But not talking at home about difficult social, political, and gospel topics can be perilous. Our silence may mean that less informed peers or the media may take our place. Sometimes parents look for "teachable moments" which may or may not come. And even when they do come, as parents, we can be dismissed if they see us as simply "correcting" misinformation. Research suggests that when parents' conversations at home are focused only on "the answers," children either stop asking or dismiss their parents' answers because they are seen as the same old stuff.

THROUGH FAMILY STORIES

Teaching our kids can be quite the challenge, but learning with them is easy. At such times, it's more about the questions we ask together than the answers we give, more about joint discovery than one-way imparting information, more about being curious than knowing the correct answer. For example, my children—and now grandchildren—enjoy a story I occasionally tell about a time when I got in trouble as an eleven-year-old boy.

---

3. Vasco Lopes, qtd. in Anna Silman, "Why Are Parents So Bad At Teaching Their Own Kids?" *The Cut,* 3 Aug. 2020, www.thecut.com/2020/08/why-are-parents-so-bad-at-teaching-their-own-kids.html.

We lived in a rural area where people often placed money on an outgoing letter in their mailbox if they did not have a stamp, relying on the letter carrier to place the correct stamp on the letter. One day my cousin and I were riding Ole Pal, my grandfather's horse, and playfully opening the lids of mailboxes as we passed by. As we flipped open a particular mailbox lid, we spied several coins inside. Thinking no one would notice, we grabbed the few coins and rode to the lone gas station and convenience store in our small town to buy treats. Neither of us felt very good about what we had done. Both of us were looking for a way to repay the person we had taken the coins from.

When I arrived home, my dad was waiting for me. Our neighbor had seen me take the coins and called my dad. Not waiting for him to talk to me, I told him what I had done and how ashamed I was of my actions. He was sympathetic but said that I needed to go to my neighbor, tell him what I had done, and ask him for jobs to repay him for my misdeed. My dad drove me to my neighbor's house and waited in the street while I confessed and asked for my neighbor's forgiveness—which he freely gave. Then, I asked for jobs that I could do to repay him for what I had done. He gave a list to me and over the next two weeks I went to his house to pull weeds, fill a watering trough for his horses, and sweep his garage. It was a lesson I never forgot.

When I share personal stories like this that show my own limitations, family members and learners in a classroom room alike seem to relate well to underlying gospel messages. Stories which show our vulnerability, our humanity, our desire to do well even when we fall short, are rich and powerful.

Sharing family stories forges connections among family members. Such stories convey the values that unite family members. They are a way of saying: "This is who we are and what we stand for." When it comes to our families and even our wards or social groups, we recognize intuitively that the stories we hold in common are an important part of "the ties that bind."

Beyond creating connections, good stories also build familiarity and trust, and allow others to enter the story where they are, making them more open to learning. Good stories can contain multiple meanings so they're surprisingly efficient in conveying important ideas in graspable ways. You just can't say too much about how good stories build family connections and engagement.

BY THE SPIRIT

President Marion G. Romney once said, "I always know when I am speaking under the inspiration of the Holy Ghost because I always learn something from what I've said."[4] He's the teacher, and suddenly he's either saying things or thinking things that he had not thought before—or if he thought them before, they have come with new delight, new power. Those might be some of the ways to get an indication you are teaching by the Spirit.

In introducing the revised two-hour block schedule in the October 2018 General Conference, Elder Quentin L. Cook concluded his remarks with this focus on conversion to Christ:

> The first page of the individual and family resource booklet points out: "The aim of all gospel learning and teaching is to deepen our conversion and help us become more like Jesus Christ. . . . This means relying on Christ to change our hearts." This is assisted by reaching "beyond a classroom into an individual's heart and home. It requires consistent, daily efforts to understand and live the gospel. True conversion requires the influence of the Holy Ghost."[5]

THROUGH SERVICE

Our homes are "learning labs," places to practice and apply gospel principles in a supportive setting.

Elder D. Todd Christofferson taught:

> This religion is not concerned only with self; rather, we are all called to serve. We are the eyes, hands, head, feet, and other members of the body of Christ, and even "those members . . . which seem to be more feeble, are necessary." We need these callings, and we need to serve.[6]

And even when we don't know what to say or how we can help, perhaps simply speaking openly about this discomfort enables us to develop the kind of charity that constitutes the "pure love of Christ."

When talking with children at the earliest possible age about the value of helping, sharing, and serving, parents are cultivating a mindset that shapes the way they view the world.

4. Marion G. Romney, qtd. in Boyd K. Packer, *Teach Ye Diligently* (Salt Lake City: Deseret Book Co., 1975), 304.
5. Quentin L. Cook, "Deep and Lasting Conversion to Heavenly Father and the Lord Jesus Christ," *Ensign,* Nov. 2019, 11.
6. D. Todd Christofferson, "Why the Church," *Ensign,* Nov. 2015, 109.

Helping others in the family also gives children a strong sense of belonging. When children are busy helping, they are less inclined to be self-centered. Teaching children "to love one another, and to serve one another" can often be an antidote for fighting and quarreling. (See Mosiah 4:14–15.)

As President Spencer W. Kimball taught, "When we are engaged in the service of our fellowmen, not only do our deeds assist them, but we put our own problems in a fresher perspective."[7]

HOME AND HOME WARD

Rather than regarding the Church and the family operating separately, the Lord intends for them to be woven together so tightly that each reinforces the other. As Elder D. Todd Christofferson notes:

> We must remember that in the beginning, the Church was the family, and even today as separate institutions, the family and the Church serve and strengthen one another. Neither supplants the other, and certainly the Church, even at its best, cannot substitute for parents.[8]

Our home ward can become like an extension of our family and serve in tandem with us as we teach each other at home. Wards and branches are not designed to replace the family unit but to support gospel learning and teaching there. A local church unit is another place where we can learn together, be vulnerable with one another, and have a kind of "safety net" to help meet our spiritual, emotional, and temporal needs.

Speaking at the general conference, Sister Virginia Pearce, then a counselor in the Young Women's General Presidency of the Church, emphasized that ward families can provide an unparalleled sense of belonging similar to a righteous home. Quoting Robert Frost's poem "Death of the Hired Man," she relates:

> Home is the place where, when you go there,
> They have to take you in.
> I should have called it
> Something you somehow haven't to deserve.

Sister Pearce then emphasizes that a ward is also "something you somehow haven't to deserve." Because we are all looking out for each other in our local ward or branch, we share various perspectives openly knowing that others will take what we say and do with kindness and forbearance.

7. Spencer W. Kimball, "Small Acts of Service," *Ensign,* Dec. 1974, 2.
8. D. Todd Christofferson, "Why the Church," *Ensign,* Nov. 2015, 110.

SUMMARY

The ultimate goal of gospel learning and teaching, whether at home or at church, is simply to help ourselves and others become more like Christ. We do this by understanding human beings as God's ultimate "service project," His divine aspiration to give us mortal experience that enables us to make the kind of choices which allow us to live in His presence. We are always His and He is always ours. He will never forsake us; and try as hard as we might, we can never really forsake Him. We are in this together.

Chapter 3

When Parents Teach

During the COVID-19 pandemic, many parents were required to teach their kids at home in new and unique ways. This included more than math and science. For the first time, many parents began asking themselves what life skills and personal habits they needed to teach their children—and what virtues and character traits mattered most that they needed to help family members acquire.

Along with asking themselves what they needed to teach, this pandemic-related environment prompted them to consider *when* the best time was to teach these important principles and habits.

Teaching in the Savior's Way emphasizes that "Most of the Savior's teaching did not happen in a synagogue but in informal, everyday settings—while eating a meal with His disciples, drawing water from a well, or walking past a fig tree."[1] Taking advantage of these informal settings and spontaneous "teaching moments" enabled Him to be "ready always" to share a gospel perspective.

This same resource notes:

> These conversations are most effective at the time the opportunity arises, not the next time the topic comes up in a manual. Because such moments are unexpected, you can't prepare for them as you

1. "Take Advantage of Spontaneous Teaching Moments," *Teaching in the Savior's Way* (The Church of Jesus Christ of Latter-day Saints, 2016), 16.

would prepare for a lesson. However, you can prepare *yourself* by being "ready always," (1 Peter 3:15) and sensitive to the Spirit.[2]

Children constantly observe how parents and other family members treat each other, how decisions are made, and how problems are solved. All the experiences children have help shape their own belief systems about themselves, the world around them, and where they fit into the scheme of things.

Learning how things work and proving ourselves is an essential purpose of earth life. In Abraham 3:24–26 we read about the purpose of this "second estate," or life on earth, is to discover and demonstrate our commitment to following God's plans.

> And we will prove them herewith, to see if they will do all things whatsoever the Lord their God will command them; (Abraham 3:25)

Proving ourselves can seem like a tall order. We often associate proving as equivalent to passing a test or going on a quest. While these are both potential ways to think about how we might prove ourselves, there may be insights from mathematical proofs that can be helpful in considering how we prove ourselves. In algebra, there are three essential characteristics of a proof:

- Following accepted processes using recognized principles, axioms, and corollaries
- Showing work to better see blind alleys, dead ends, and the way forward
- Revising assumptions when stuck or uncertain

In this light, *proving* ourselves to our Heavenly Father takes on a different meaning. Rather than striving to pass a test—with all of the stress and anxiety that implies—or perhaps thinking we must find some heroic thing to do, we can instead think of *proving* ourselves as intentionally and rigorously deciding what is important—our real, eternal priorities—then showing our work by how we live. Lastly, we eliminate things that distract us, obscure our intentions, or take us in a wrong direction.

With this background, we can now recognize that teaching and learning are less about acquiring new information and more about becoming adept at decision-making, less about rote memorization and more about alignment with fundamental gospel principles, and much less about telling someone what to do and much more about letting them experience things for ourselves.

2. Ibid.

This decision-making approach applies equally to young Primary children as well as older adults, to uncertain teenagers as much as endowed temple workers, to experienced missionaries and to their new investigators. It is at the heart of the Prophet Joseph's oft-quoted statement: "I teach them correct principles and they govern themselves."[3] While classes and ages and circumstances vary, the *discovery learning process* is flexible enough to fit any situation.

Like an algebraic proof, teaching itself is a rigorous process of making many new discoveries. It is so much more than sprinkling a few quotes or scriptures and then asking family members for their thoughts. It is constantly discovering, planning, acting, and reflecting as outlined in "A Pattern for Growth" in the Church's *Personal Development: Youth Guidebook.*

TELLING ISN'T TEACHING

Picture this: a parent is at the front of a living room with a megaphone while family members have their earbuds and iPods securely in place. An exaggeration? Maybe. What's the remedy? Teachers or parents may say to eliminate all competing distractions. Certainly, there are many "weapons of mass distraction" in the world today. But rather than simply oppose them, can families learn instead how to leverage them? When and how can distractions themselves become the "main attraction"? When and how can distractions inform our experiences and reorient family members' thoughts, actions, and mindsets?

Since so many people think that teaching is talking or telling, they may also think that learning must simply be listening. Consequently, when class or family members are not listening, teachers or parents think they need to talk louder. When talking louder doesn't get results, they blame others: leaders, schools, parents, society. This is not to say there aren't some very real distractions that make learning difficult—impossible, in some cases—but the cause is not always in others and the remedy isn't always for someone else to fix it. Sometimes, it is how we think about gospel teaching and learning itself that needs to be reconsidered and thereby our role and mission as parents and teachers could benefit from some redefinition.

Real gospel teaching requires an understanding of the learning process. To begin with, a home is not a stadium with the announcer trying to be heard over the crowd noise. Nor is it a performance at Lincoln Center to a subdued, appreciative audience. Gospel teaching is not the efficient

3. "Leading in the Lord's Way," *Teachings of Presidents of the Church: Joseph Smith* (The Church of Jesus Christ of Latter-day Saints, 2007), 284.

delivery of new information. Instead, it is understanding the learner's needs and circumstances so precisely that we "let [our] words tend to edifying one another" (D&C 136: 24). This will help us connect with the Holy Ghost—who will bring all things to our remembrance—including our pre-earth life, our divine potential, and the spiritual legacy bequeathed by our Heavenly Parents.

LETTING IN, GETTING IN

Gospel teaching and learning together starts with *joining up.* We choose to enlist, to get started, to go together. Like early pioneer scouting expeditions, the terrain can be uncertain and maybe a little or a lot different than expected. Yet, despite having a general idea of the needed direction, it still takes common consent to make regular progress each day. Even wagon trains rely on shared agreement, not merely giving and receiving orders as many pioneer histories and records show.

John the Revelator offered a similar perspective when he told us the Savior waits to be invited in and never forces Himself to be heard.

> Behold, I stand at the door, and knock; if any man will hear my voice, and open the door, I will come in to him, and will sup with him, and he with me. (Revelation 3:20)

Just as the Savior must be let in, so parents must be invited in by family who must decide to open the door for them. It cannot be forced. It is a two-way process of knocking and opening. This is, according to Elder Richard G. Scott, "an exercise in agency that permits the Holy Ghost to communicate a personalized message suited to their individual needs." Elder Scott then explained, "Creating an atmosphere of participation enhances the probability that the Spirit will teach more important lessons than you can communicate."[4]

CHOICE AND ACCOUNTABILITY

The Young Women's theme emphasizes the importance of choice and accountability. This happens best in families when family members are included in conversations that establish family rules. When parents impose limits without their kids' input, they are setting them up to be resentful and incentivizing them to find ways to "beat the system."

4. Richard F. Scott, "To Learn and to Teach More Effectively," Brigham Young University Campus Education Week devotional, 21 Aug. 2007, speeches.byu.edu.

This "common consent" approach is no guarantee of complete domestic harmony. In fact, most likely there will be some pointed discussions about family rules which could include the role of technology and the amount of screen time family members are allotted. But it's only when kids agree and then begin to monitor their own behavior that they learn the skills they need to navigate the world—especially since parents aren't always around.

Edward Deci and Richard Ryan, researchers at the University of Rochester, have spent decades studying human motivation and family development. Their approach to developing self-determination and independence has three major ingredients for children to grow and develop:

- *Competence*: sense of confidence in getting results when exerting effort
- *Autonomy*: ability to make choices consistent with learned values and interests
- *Relatedness*: feeling cared for and a sense of belonging with others

To develop these three capabilities, they suggest doing the following:

1. *Nurture inner motivational capacities*: find ways to build on children's interests, preferences, competencies, and choices.
2. *Avoid external regulators* like sticker charts, special treats, generic praise, competitions, or extra screen time simply to get compliance.
3. *Use non-controlling language*: make observations and focus on statements that are informational:
    - "I see that you . . ."
    - "I notice that you . . ."
    - "Would you be willing to . . ."
4. *Provide a rationale for doing things*: in other words, explain why something needs to be done now or in a certain way.
5. *Acknowledge and accept expressions of negative emotions:* sometimes your child will not like family rules, boundaries, or requests. There will be conflicts between required limits and your child's preferences. Acknowledge the negative emotions, avoid statements like "just get in the car!" but persist in implementing boundaries.

MORAL AGENCY AND PERSONAL DECISION-MAKING

In commenting on changes made in the Youth and Sunday School curriculum, Matthew O. Richardson, then Second Counselor in the General Sunday School Presidency, remarked:

> Some still think "Come, Follow Me" is about boosting class participation, getting people to talk. No, it's an invitation to act, to exercise agency. You can do that in many ways. A person can exercise her agency to listen, to share, to ask questions, to respond. All of those are ways that bring blessings for action.[5]

Parents who engage family members in addressing difficult life experiences through real-time activities increase both this agency to act and the relevance of classroom discussions. Rich gospel discussions go beyond reciting facts or reviewing lists.

As far back as 1991, President Russell M. Nelson urged families to create robust interactions with each other by regularly considering problematic situations and then making conscious choices about what to do and how to do it. For instance, commenting on Sabbath observance, then Elder Nelson said:

> I plead with you to do more than passively follow lists of dos and don'ts compiled by others. Generate your own policies and live by them.[6]

The process of deciding together what to do in difficult or problematic situations after reviewing what is taught in the scriptures strengthens everyone's resolve. We make better decisions when we have a chance to "talk out" sticky situations and then make a personal decision about what we will "go and do."

People want to connect together—not just for rallies or socials—but to create ties that facilitate sharing and caring. This type of classroom environment is perhaps what is envisioned by Doctrine & Covenants 88:122.

> Appoint among yourselves a teacher, and let not all be spokesman at once; but let each one speak at a time and let all listen unto his sayings, that when all have spoken that all may be edified of all, and that every man may have an equal privilege.

Whenever anyone accepts an invitation to act, they are exercising their moral agency and when doing so, real learning occurs. Teaching is not simply telling or even discussing a topic. It is, in fact, more about intentionally helping someone decide to do something in a very purposeful way. It is like using a map to explore unfamiliar terrain. We find our way by reading

5. Matthew O. Richardson, qtd. in Tad Walch, "Shaking up Sunday School: 'Revolution' in LDS teaching seeks to activate learners," *Deseret News*, 28 Sept. 2016, www.deseret.com
6. Russell M. Nelson, "Standards of Standard-Bearers of the Lord," Brigham Young University fireside address, 6 Jan. 1991, speeches.byu.edu.

an accurate map and then exploring together with the Holy Ghost as our guide who "will show unto you all things what you should do" (2 Nephi 32:5). As Elder Matthew O. Richardson further taught:

> Parents who mirror the workings of the Holy Ghost create homes where families learn to value rather than just learn about values. In like manner, rather than just learning about doctrines, teachers help learners understand and live gospel doctrines. The Holy Ghost is unrestrained as individuals exercise *their* agency appropriately.[7]

"Families learn to value" only when parents facilitate children's decision-making. This requires observing, probing, demonstrating, de-briefing and choosing so that the Holy Ghost can enable us feel, and choose to do next. Such real teaching is so much more than talking and discussing. It is instead jointly engaging in exploring gospel principles and gospel living. When done together, both teacher and learners are making new discoveries.

RECOGNIZE INDIVIDUAL LEARNING STYLES

There are four main styles of learning: visual (sight), auditory (hearing), tactile (touch), and kinesthetic (movement). Recognizing these differences is fundamental in "reaching the one" while also teaching the "ninety and nine." It's unnecessary to pick and choose one learning style over another when using each of these four methods provides variety as well as ways to access the hearts and minds of all participants.

When considering family members' learning styles, start by recognizing the fundamental difference between introverts and extroverts. Introverts generally prefer answering questions by writing answers rather than verbally jumping in and discussing them. Extroverts, of course, prefer saying things that come to mind at that moment. Recognizing these differences between introverts and extroverts, instructors can use Post-It notes or written thought questions to engage introverts and balance such "question asking" with more traditional discussion questions.

Keep in mind that appealing to all four learning styles—visual, auditory, tactile, and kinesthetic—creates a lively learning environment with a broad appeal to adults, teens, and younger children.

The scriptures show examples of how to incorporate these learning styles both at church and in the home. Here's one example:

7. Matthew O. Richardson, "Teaching After the Manner of the Spirit," *Ensign*, Nov. 2011, 95.

> Therefore shall ye lay up these my words in your heart and in your soul, and bind them for a sign upon your head, that they may be as frontlets between your eyes.
>
> And ye shall teach them to your children, speaking of them when thou sittest in thine house, and when thou walkest by the way, when thou liest down, and when thou risest up.
>
> And thou shalt write them upon the door posts of thine house, and upon thy gates. (Deuteronomy 11:18–20)

Notice the variety of ways the scriptures are used to teach, remember, and apply a message: binding them on our hands like a bracelet so we can literally touch them, talking and listening about them informally in ordinary circumstances throughout the day, and putting them on a wreath at the front door or on a wall in a room in the house as visible reminders.

Here are some additional suggestions that can help parents teach gospel principles in each of these learning styles.

- *Visual.* Use Church-produced videos and social media messages. Hang pictures of the temple around the house and use them often in classroom instruction. Ask class or family members to illustrate a story from the scriptures.
- *Auditory.* Consider making dramatic readings of key events from the scriptures or use segments from audiobooks as both a change of pace and to heighten attention.
- *Tactile.* Use visual objects to engage participants and promote application. Create lessons or learning activities with a mustard seed, sea salt, lamps filled with oil, unleavened bread, and the like.
- *Kinesthetic.* Use realistic discovery-learning activities including simulations, structured exercises, role plays, case studies, and the like.

Using methods that include all four learning styles allows both teachers and learners to engage as many of the physical senses as possible. Like any method or tool, the more it is used, the more familiar it will become for either a teacher or parent.

FAMILY COUNCILS

Elder M. Russell Ballard has encouraged Church members to hold regular family councils and use them to listen, plan, and learn from each other. He has said: "A family council, when conducted with love and with Christlike attributes, will counter the impact of modern technology that often distracts us from spending quality time with each other and also tends to bring evil right into our homes."[8]

With so many distractions in the world today— electronic and social media included—many educators and researchers have noted that perhaps the most important skill that parents can help their children acquire is the ability to become *indistractable.*

There are distractions all around us—things that we do without really thinking about it when bored or impatient or simply waiting for someone or something. While scrolling Facebook or aimlessly reviewing old texts are often cited as primary distractions, a distraction is anything that we do *unintentionally.* Family councils help us better determine what we want to do *on purpose* with our unscheduled or unallocated time and thereby minimize unwanted distractions in our lives.

Elder Ballard quotes the Church pamphlet *Our Family,* which states, "This council can meet to discuss family problems, work out finances, make plans, support and strengthen [each other,] and pray for one another and for the family unit." He emphasizes that family councils are not a time for parents to distribute a list of "to do's" or complaints about things that are not getting done around the house. Instead, parents can and should use family councils for discussions and problem-solving, which can mean that solutions are developed that they may never have considered previously.

Describing his own experience, Elder Ballard said, "I found that when the list came out, it turned the children off. So I tried bringing up a specific problem—such as the garden needs weeding—and then simply asked the family, 'What can we do about it? What are your ideas?'"[9]

Everyone wants to be part of a family; it's a basic human need. Family councils promote such belonging and connectedness when all family members participate and are able to share ideas. Getting started can be tricky for first timers especially if older teenagers see it as a way simply to get them to do things they are not used to doing, but it's worth the effort. Here's some tips for getting started:

- *Keep it short:* Family council meetings should be less than 30 minutes. Even if there are more things to discuss, keeping it short subliminally encourages everyone to join in next time knowing it's not going to last long. As the old phrase goes: "Keep them wanting something more."

8. M. Russell Ballard, "Family Councils," *Ensign*, May 2016, 63.
9. "Family Councils: A Conversation with Elder and Sister Ballard," *Ensign*, June 2003.

- *Stay upbeat:* Find ways to recognize the good things family members are doing for each other; ways they are helpful or positive or encouraging to one another.
- *Don't over plan:* Family councils have their purpose, but they are not the only way to communicate with each other; be willing to be flexible and spontaneous.
- *Don't try to control participation:* Sometimes parents try too hard to get everyone's input; ask open-ended questions but don't force comments from family members.
- *Meet regularly:* While initial family councils may feel awkward or forced, keep at it; the more you do it—and the more family members expect it—the more dynamic and beneficial they will become.

Among the benefits of family councils are the communication and connection that naturally flow from them. Elder Ballard notes that "the Lord has provided a way to counter the invasion of negative technology that can distract us from spending quality time with each other. He has done this by providing the council system to strengthen, protect, safeguard, and nurture our most precious relationships."[10]

SUMMARY

If we begin with the end in mind, we'll never lose track of our ultimate purpose to help family members "come unto Christ" by hearing and heeding His call to return to our celestial home. While family members must do their own part, there is much that parents can do to inspire, support, encourage, motivate, and assist them in deciding to choose this path.

10. M. Russell Ballard, "Family Councils," *Ensign*, May 2016, 65.

Chapter 4

Where Parents Teach

Parents have many opportunities throughout the day to influence, guide, and provide new experiences to other family members. Sometimes this happens deliberately such as teaching a Family Home Evening lesson while at other times it happens casually, such as comparison shopping at a store.

PARENTS AS ROLE MODELS

It's well-established that parents are their children's most important role models. Even as they become teenagers and look more toward their peers for acceptance and validation, family members still watch, listen to, and learn from what parents *do* as much as what they may *say*.

Beyond attending church meetings together, at any age parents can influence family members' values and develop Christlike attributes through action, reflection, and joint planning. It doesn't take a lesson or a meeting—although they can also be helpful—but rather intentionally acting consistent with the values and attributes parents want their children to develop.

For example, if parents want their children to learn gratitude and thoughtfulness, they can let their children see them write thank you notes. If they want to teach friendliness, they can talk to people standing in the grocery line. If they want to teach patience, they can make the most of longer than normal wait times while on a telephone hold, rather than express exasperation.

Telling each other real stories about "lived experiences" allows children both to "see and do" similar things in their own lives. Recently, this incident in the life of one of my grandson's has made the rounds not only in our own extended family but in other families as well. More than inspiration, it has become motivation in giving others the courage to act on their good intentions. Here is one such story:

> Rowan squinted as the teacher beckoned to a new boy to come to the front of the class.
>
> "This is Ernest," she said. "He just arrived here in Hawaii from a country called Ukraine. He doesn't speak any English. Will you make friends with him?"
>
> Several class members nodded their heads. But at recess, Ernest went off by himself. He was the only one in class wearing long pants and a long sleeved shirt. He looked sad. Rowan wanted to make friends with him, but he didn't know what to say.
>
> When he arrived home after school, Rowan asked his Dad to help him turn on the Alexa smart speaker they had. Rowan then asked Alexa how to saw "it's lunchtime" in Ukrainian. The smart speaker said "obidniy chas." Rowan tried saying that several times, but it was difficult for him. So, he asked the smart speaker to tell him how to say "hello" in Ukrainian. "Pryvet," it said. That seemed easier. He asked the smart speaker to repeat it while Rowan said it over and over.
>
> At school during recess, Rowan found the new boy sitting alone again. He stood next to him and, smiling, said in a loud voice: "Pryvit!" The boy smiled back and gave Rowan a gummy bear. Rowan sat next to him and said "pryvet" again. Then, Rowan said "Hello." Slowly, the new boy said "Hello" back to Rowan who nodded his head in agreement. The new boy gave Rowan another gummy bear. Next, Rowan drew a tic-tac-toe grid and showed the boy how to play. Sometimes the new boy drew 2 or 3 x's without giving Rowan a turn, but Rowan didn't care. He wanted to make friends more than he wanted to win the game. They walked and played together at recess every day that week.
>
> Later, Rowan's Dad asked him about the new boy. His name is "Ernest," Rowan said triumphantly. "We play games together and he gives me gummy bears." His Dad smiled. "You are a good friend," his Dad said. "Ernest is a refugee from a country far away from us. President Nelson has said that Jesus was a refugee as a boy and asked us to be friends when we meet people from other countries. What do you think it takes to be a friend?"
>
> "It takes a tiny bit of love and finding a game to play together," Rowan said. "Then, others can join in and play the game too and talk and get to know each other." His Dad gave Rowan a hug. "You are following Jesus and doing what the prophet asks us to do," he said. "Now, Ernest is no longer a stranger. He is your friend."

Almost nothing reinforces these positive values quite like simply being available. Often, just being there shows family members that as parents you are interested in them and their activities. For years, a friend wore a lapel button that said simply "Showing Up is 90% of life." Of course, this requires being emotionally there, not just continuing to work offline from the office or texting colleagues and friends about future activities.

These days, while some parents attend all of their children's sports and extracurricular activities, others wonder if it's necessary or worth it to spend hours in the stands when they are not even with their children. Sports psychologist Richard Ginsburg addresses this and other questions in his book *Whose Game Is It, Anyway: A Guide to Helping Your Child Get the Most from Sports.* In his research, he found that more than 90% of children ages 7–14 wanted their parents to attend games and other related activities with them even if they did not play much nor interact during these games or events. Children see parents' attendance at games and recitals as signs of interest, caring, and support in addition to whatever actual time they may spend together with them.[1]

ELECTRONICS AND SOCIAL MEDIA

It is the digital age. Smart phones and gaming devices are here to stay. So, the question is not whether, but how and when family members use devices to communicate, play, learn, and share.

Surveys show that tweens and teens are using electronic devices more and more: an average of five and a half hours a day for tweens (ages 8–12 years) and an average of eight and a half hours a day for teens (ages 13–18 years) according to a nationwide survey conducted by Common Sense Media.[2]

Researchers and other experts emphasize that not all screen time is unproductive and that digital devices can function like any tool or modern convenience to be helpful or hurtful, relieve stress or create it, teach and inspire or diminish and exclude. Roughly, the experts say, there are two types of "screen time":

- *productive screen time*: working, learning, connecting with friends, and problem-solving games

1. Richard D. Ginsburg, Stephen Durant, and Amy Baltzell, *Whose Game Is It, Anyway? A Guide to Helping Your Child Get the Most from Sports, Organized by Age and Stage* (Houghton Mifflin Company, 2006).
2. W. Rideout, A. Peebles, S. Mann, & M. B. Robb, *Common Sense census: Media use by tweens and teens, 2021* (San Francisco, CA: Common Sense, 2022), 3.

- *consuming screen time:* watching shows, scrolling Facebook or Instagram, and casual or battle video games

Researchers such as Jean Twenge and Delany Ruston say that more than two hours per day spent on consuming screen time significantly affects tweens and teens attention, focus, and memory. Dr. Jean Twenge, author of *iGen: Why Today's Super-Connected Kids are Growing Up Less Rebellious, More Tolerant, Less Happy—and Completely Unprepared for Adulthood—and What That Means for the Rest of Us* has found that tweens and teens may begin to have less self-control, less emotional stability, less curiosity, and a greater inability to finish tasks when consuming screen time drives out play, reading, and interpersonal interaction.[3]

While not a complete antidote, Dr. Twenge recommends that parents and their children discuss and agree on how much and what kind of screen time will be permitted among all family members. Related to this joint determination, how consuming screen time will be monitored is also a critical element. There are lots of available apps to help monitor screen time if parents and children decide to utilize them. Discussing results regularly at family council or during other family discussions can also be helpful.

INQUIRING MINDS WANT TO KNOW

Elder Kim B. Clark has urged us to go beyond superficial understanding of spiritual things by making deep learning a lifelong goal.

> The learning that allows each of you to rise "to the full stature of your divine potential" is what I will call *deep learning:* learning of the whole soul—the mind, the heart, the body, and the immortal spirit. Deep learning applies to every kind of knowledge, whether spiritual or secular. Learning is deep when it increases your power to do three things: (1) to know and understand; (2) to take effective, righteous action; and (3) to become more like our Heavenly Father.[4]

If we are curious, we are never bored. We will always want to know more, to pull aside the curtain and to discover more. Curiosity is all about the questions we ask. Not silly or irrelevant questions. Instead, questions that help us to think, grow, experience, and discover. Developing the ability to ask inspiring questions starts with curiosity.

3. Jean M. Twenge, *iGen: Why Today's Super-Connected Kids are Growing Up Less Rebellious, More Tolerant, Less Happy—and Completely Unprepared for Adulthood—and What That Means for the Rest of Us* (Atria Books, 2017).
4. Kim B. Clark "Learning for the Whole Soul," *Ensign*, Aug. 2017.

The Prophet Joseph Smith taught:

> *Thy mind, O man! if thou wilt lead a soul unto salvation, must stretch as high as the utmost heavens, and search into and contemplate the lowest considerations of the darkest abyss, and the broad expanse of eternity—thou must commune with God.*5

Note that to lead a soul upward, it is sometimes necessary to "search into and contemplate the darkest abyss," where many souls are trapped. But also note that the intent of searching the abyss is ultimately to lead souls heavenward to salvation—that is to edify—not to sojourn in the abyss or to revel in darkness.

COUNTER BOREDOM WITH VARIETY

Despite our best efforts, parents often hear kids say: "I'm bored." So, trying to be helpful, we may find ourselves offering suggestion after suggestion only to get rejection after rejection. In frustration, we may even give up.

While youth may voice it more often and more openly, even older adults get easily bored nowadays, according to researchers who are studying boredom. These researchers note that boredom at home or in a classroom stem principally from sameness and predictability. The antidote? Variety and novelty. Do something different, or in a different way. Find a new approach. Give up the "same old, same old" way of doing things. Ask questions that help family members learn.

This may sound good, but how can you do it as a parent? Through inspiring questions that go beyond the obvious and engage children's curiosity. This means starting with what interests them: sports, clothes, work, family. What's on their mind: what unanswered questions are they hardly even aware of that they would like to discuss with an interested parent who is going to respect "their space" and their moral agency? How can you "drill down" on a topic so that you go beyond the expected, the predictable, and find something new? How can you help family members be *awed* and *enlightened*?

In the book of Proverbs, these relationships are further illustrated:

> So that thou incline thine ear unto wisdom, *and* apply thine heart to understanding;
>
> Yea, if thou criest after knowledge, *and* liftest up thy voice for understanding;

5. *Teaching of Presidents of the Church: Joseph Smith* (2011), 267.

> If thou seekest her as silver, and searchest for her as *for* hid treasures;
> Then shalt thou understand the fear of the Lord, and find the knowledge of God.
> For the Lord giveth wisdom: out of his mouth *cometh* knowledge and understanding.
> He layeth up sound wisdom for the righteous: *he is* a buckler to them that walk uprightly.
> He keepeth the paths of judgment, and preserveth the way of his saints.
> Then shalt thou understand righteousness, and judgment, and equity; *yea,* every good path. (Proverbs 2:2–9)

MEDITATE TO GAIN INSIGHTS

While we don't use the term "meditate" often, it is used regularly in the scriptures and by Church leaders—more than two dozen times in the scriptures alone. President David O. McKay once said:

> We pay too little attention to the value of meditation, a principle of devotion. . . . Meditation is the language of the soul. It is defined as "a form of private devotion, or spiritual exercise, consisting in deep, continued reflection on some religious theme." Meditation is a form of prayer. . . . Meditation is one of the most secret, most sacred doors through which we pass into the presence of the Lord.[6]

Pam Blackwell, a meditation expert who teaches at Brigham Young University and author of *Christ—Centered Meditation: A Handbook for Spiritual Practice,* put it this way:

> I think meditation is the major tool to enhancing our connection with our Heavenly Father, Jesus, and the Holy Spirit. I spend a lot more time during the day in a relaxed, receptive spiritual state. . . . If I'm prayerful about something, I am much more aware of the answers all around me. I live in a pretty joyous state; I'm in a good mood—a "God mood."[7]

To some members of the Church, the word "meditate" may be associated with Eastern religions or fringe groups, but it has a different connotation in the Bible and among practicing members of the Church than may be commonly used today. Bible scholars note the word is better associated with

6. *Teachings of Presidents of the Church: David O. McKay* (2011), 31–32.
7. "Faithful Meditation," *Latter-day Saints Channel,* 7 Apr. 2015, www.churchofjesuschrist.org/inspiration/faithful-meditation.

study, reflection, musings, and mulling over a specific passage of scripture or gospel concept. It is not aimless. Even the Prophet Joseph Smith wrote that prior to the First Vision he often thought deeply about what others were saying about religion along with their interpretation of the Bible:

> During this time of great excitement my mind was caught up in serious reflection and great uneasiness; . . . my feelings were deep and often poignant . . . (JS—H 1:8)

In Genesis 24:63 we read the first use of the term "meditate" in the Bible when Issac found a quiet place to reflect and pray:

> And Isaac went out to meditate in the field at the eventide . . .

Later, in a more direct way, Moses tells Joshua to meditate on the word of the Lord and let us know that mediation is purposeful and used in better understanding the scriptures and how to apply them in our lives:

> This book of the law shall not depart out of thy mouth; but thou shalt meditate therein day and night, that thou mayest observe to do according to all that is written therein: for then thou shalt make thy way prosperous, and then thou shalt have good success. (Joshua 1:8)

We can realize the benefits of meditation and come closer to our Heavenly Father if we follow three simple steps:

Set ourselves before the Lord: In the same way that we might anticipate watching a majestic sunset or the view from a mountaintop after a strenuous hike, we can begin meditating by anticipating arriving in His presence.

> Then said he unto me, Fear not, Daniel: for from the first day that thou didst set thine heart to understand, and to chasten thyself before thy God, thy words were heard, and I am come for thy words. (Daniel 10:12)

Dwell on the good things from God: reflect on what Heavenly Father has done for you and others. Make a mental list.

> And be not conformed to this world: but be ye transformed by the renewing of your mind, that ye may prove what is that good, and acceptable, and perfect, will of God. (Romans 12:2)

Believe: There is an old saying that reminds us: "Simply believe: do not the leaves fall down just like that?" In the end, it comes down to believing. Choose to believe and mediation will become a rich and endearing way to seek and obtain the Lord's guidance in your life and storehouse to draw from for many, many gospel insights.

> And straightway the father of the child cried out, and said with tears, Lord, I believe; help thou my unbelief. (Mark 9:24)

When we are at our wit's end, when we don't know what else to do, if we will simply turn to our Heavenly Father, He will be there for us. At such times, we can "Be still and know that I am God" (D&C 101:16).

SEEK TO BE TAUGHT BY THE HOLY GHOST

Whether during family *Come, Follow Me* discussions or Family Home Evening lessons, President Gordon B. Hinckley said this about the importance of good teaching:

> Eternal life will come only as men and women are *taught with such effectiveness* that they change and discipline their lives. They cannot be coerced into righteousness or into heaven. They must be led, and that means teaching.[8]

This occurs when we partner with the Holy Ghost in teaching. As Nephi emphasized, "When a man speaketh by the power of the Holy Ghost the power of the Holy Ghost carrieth it unto the hearts of the children of men" (2 Nephi 33:1).

Inviting the Spirit into our daily lives is powerful and increases our ability to receive direction and feel its presence. Elder David A. Bednar taught:

> We more readily receive and recognize the Spirit of the Lord as we appropriately invite Him into our lives. We cannot compel, coerce, or command the Holy Ghost. Rather, we should invite Him into our lives with the same gentleness and tenderness by which He entreats us.[9]

SHARING FAMILY STORIES

When He was on earth, the Savior taught through stories. Instead of simply telling people they should love their neighbors, He told the story of the Good Samaritan; instead of merely stating that God is loving and forgiving, He told the parable of the Prodigal Son; instead of just reminding us that He cares for each individual, He told about the Good Shepherd and the lost sheep. These stories not only contain gospel truths but telling them allows the Holy Ghost to teach and testify to family members.

---

8. Gordon B. Hinckley, qtd. in Jeffrey R. Holland, "A Teacher Come from God," *Ensign,* May 1998, 26.
9. David A. Bednar, "Receive the Holy Ghost," *Ensign,* Nov. 2010, 96.

Decades of research have shown that resilient families communicate effectively through shared experiences and sharing family stories about important virtues and attributes. This means telling relatable stories that family members can identify with. When faced with a challenge, resilient families just add a new chapter to their life story that shows them overcoming the hardship. This skill is particularly important for children, whose identity tends to get locked in during adolescence.

The bottom line: if you want a cohesive family that knows how to handle difficulties and grow from them, then create, refine, and retell the story of your family's positive moments and your ability to bounce back from adverse ones. This becomes your legacy, what your family stands for. It is the story that makes the point about what kind of family you are. That alone may increase the odds that your family will thrive for many generations to come.

For instance, my wife's family has a legacy of persistence embodied in a famous story in their heritage that was memorialized by Ronald Reagan in 1953 when he was host of the TV series "Death Valley Days." The sixteenth episode of the series featured David Cannon and his wife Wilhelmina or "Willie" as she was called. The Cannons were called by Brigham Young in 1861 to help settle St. George, Utah as part of the Cotton Mission. But Willie hated the hot, dry desert, and pleaded constantly to return to Salt Lake City.

"Everything is so ugly here," she complained. "If you can show me just one beautiful thing in this place, I will make myself content and stop complaining."

David went up into the mountains and returned with a beautiful three-petaled blossom with delicate colors. Willie honestly admitted both to David and herself that it was indeed a thing of beauty. She never again complained but went to work with her husband to make things work in St. George where they lived for the rest of their lives.

This story is easily relatable to anyone who has traveled to the area. While the Red Rocks can be breathtaking, summers in St. George can be fierce with temperatures most days above 100 degrees Fahrenheit. Air conditioning and available water today makes living in the area starkly different than during pioneer days. It is an immensely relatable story.

INVITATIONS TO ACT

Family and gospel discussions are the most effective when there is an invitation to act included in a story, a discussion, an experience. Invitations to act can be informal and implied as well as planned and structured. There are many different ways to invite others to act. Most of all, they must be heartfelt and meaningful; consistent with the discussion that leads up to them and not coming out of left field. Simply going through the motions and offering an obligatory invitation at the end of a discussion will not only fall flat but can even be off-putting. There is no "script" that can make every invitation effective, but there are some principles and tips that, if used, will help them hit the mark.

There is much that we can learn from today's problem-solving, role playing, or "thinking electronic games," which are very "ask oriented" by the very nature of the game. They almost compel the user to explore options, process information, and draw conclusions. They have no hesitation in inviting the gamer to act.

After telling the parable of the Good Samaritan, the Savior concluded simply by saying, "Go and do thou likewise." This simple invitation both promoted the moral agency of the listeners and invited them in a very direct way to follow the example of the role model He presented in the parable. Without demanding compliance, He presented an option and then showed how this alternative could be pursued.

Fundamental to any invitations that we might extend to others is a willingness to accept whatever response they may have without taking "no" personally. If we truly believe in moral agency, we must be open to whatever response we may get when we extend invitations to act—especially for our family members. If we pout or complain that others don't follow through when we extend invitations, we are taking responsibility for their actions rather than letting them remain as "agents unto themselves."

Too easily we can get into an ego clash when extending invitations. Really, it's not about us. Be brief and direct. Avoid crowding or backing others into a corner. Give others permission to accept, reject, modify, or postpone any invitations that you offer.

While follow up is nearly always helpful, it can turn into nagging if viewed as merely checking up. Timing matters. While it may be difficult to find the right time (and place), sometimes it's important to "slow down in order to speed up." Patience is more than a virtue; it's a necessity. Don't adhere to a rigid schedule even if it is part of what may have been included in the original invitation to act. It's not merely demoralizing, it's demeaning.

The hard part about following up on invitations to act is giving up being in control. Especially for those we care about, we may closely see how they could improve "if only they would listen to us." That's a tell-tale sign of nagging. Don't give up, just look for other ways to engage and re-evaluate progress.

Chapter 5

What Parents Teach Best—A Toolbox

What parents *do* matters. Children learn from what parents and other family members *do*: how they treat a store clerk, the letter carrier, a neighbor. They also learn from what parents *say* about these people. These interactions are all part of the way family members *experience* the world. Both spontaneous and scheduled experiences comprise how families learn.

We learn by doing. It is through our experiences that we develop competencies, connections, and Christlike attributes. Our experiences also help us create conceptual maps about "how things really work" in the world along with our place in it.

There are thirty different activities or "structured experiences" in this chapter tied to specific attributes, skills, mindsets, and competencies. These skills and attributes are based on gospel principles as well as surveys among children and families about what is most needed today in families. These thirty "activity chapters" include games, simulations, role plays, structured exercises, problem-solving activities, and case studies.

A family's values may include kindness, honesty, integrity, respect for others, hard work, resilience, and more. But how these terms are discussed, applied, and experienced makes all the difference between whether they are simply platitudes or firm guideposts for daily living. Each of the following thirty chapters describe key ingredients in developing particular Christlike attributes and personal mindsets along with accompanying skills and competencies for taking action in various situations.

In the Church's *Children's Guidebook* and *Youth Guidebook,* there is a distinctive "Pattern for Growth" presented which utilizes these same elements of the discovery-learning process. It emphasizes that "you will learn from your experiences, especially when you rely on Jesus Christ and His Atonement." This "pattern for growth" includes these four often overlooked elements stressed in the guidebook:

Discover: identifying spiritual habits to change or improve
Plan: creating ways to develop a habit or personal quality
Act: noticing what does and doesn't work and why
Reflect: debriefing activities to promote learning and growth[1]

Exercises in the next section of this book follow the standard pattern described in the Church's guidebook but give more detail on what, when, and how life skills can be taught and learned.

Like a recipe book, the exercises in this section are better used and not intended just to be read. They provide scaffolding for family learning activities. Modify them to fit your family and your unique circumstances: just as a chef would modify a recipe to fit a special occasion or the tastes of a particular clientele.

Learning life skills can be more effective when adopting these basic principles and applying them using discovery learning methods. Whether learning critical thinking skills (such as analyzing world events or a math problem), or developing psychomotor skills (such as fixing a faucet or cooking over an open fire), or acquiring Christlike attributes (such as temperance, brotherly kindness, charity, humility or diligence) we learn best when we share experiences in a safe home environment that emphasizes deep learning.

We are part of a family because that is the best possible "learning lab" available on earth. In families, we have an ongoing connection to others who care about us and are interested in our growth. Through collaboration, interaction, and sharing, family members can "dig deeper" together in developing both a personal narrative and a shared bond that lasts even longer than a lifetime.

1. *Personal Development: Youth Guidebook* (The Church of Jesus Christ of Latter-day Saints, 2019), 7–15, churchofjesuschrist.org.

#1

Developing a Growth Mindset

WE ALL HAVE BELIEFS ABOUT OUR ABILITIES, OUR LIMITATIONS, OUR CAPACity to learn, and our potential to grow. These beliefs constitute our mindset which can become so powerful they influence our emotions, our spirituality, and our personality. Our mindset shapes our everyday lives and is how we interpret what happens to us and our beliefs about why such things occur.

Dr. Carol Dweck at Stanford University has studied mindsets among individuals and families and determined that people tend to adopt either a *growth mindset* or a *fixed mindset.*[1] Research shows that a growth mindset can be acquired at any age and taught under almost any circumstances.

A growth mindset occurs when we believe our abilities can be improved upon and enhanced through understanding, practice, and effort. A willingness to try new things, an inclination to view mistakes as natural and part of the learning process, and a capacity to dispassionately discuss events by withholding judgment are all basic to a growth mindset. In contrast, a fixed mindset occurs when we believe we can't change, failure is inevitable, and "this is just the way that I am." When stuck in a fixed mindset, we fear new things, stay in our comfort zone, become defensive discussing mistakes, and may feel the need to constantly prove ourselves.

While many of us are familiar with these differences between a growth and a fixed mindset, sometimes it's difficult teaching them to others or utilizing them in our families. In addition, we may have a growth mindset in some areas and a fixed mindset in other areas. Often, we have fixed mindset

1. Carol S. Dweck, *Mindset: The New Psychology of Success* (Random House Publishing, 2007).

triggers that if we can recognize when they occur, we can do something about them. Awareness is the first step toward making changes.

There is an important principle called *substitution* or thought replacement that can be utilized when teaching a growth mindset. Essentially, substitution means that we can learn to replace negative or self-limiting thoughts with more useful, developmental thoughts.

While we can have many thoughts "flash" through our brains, we can only "hold" one thought at a time. This well-established psychological principle means that our mindsets are not fixed, but instead very pliable. When we are actively making new "distinctions"—observing, noticing, discerning—rather than merely relying on habitual categorizations, we can substitute old judgments for more up-to-date and accurate conclusions. When that happens, real learning and greater self-awareness occurs.

The key to developing a growth mindset is to recognize when limiting triggers occur and substitute instead more accurate beliefs about our abilities.

Here's some examples:

Instead of:	**Substitute:**
"This is too hard."	"I can break this down more to get it."
"I always make the same mistake."	"I'm going to figure this out."
"I can't do this."	"I haven't gotten this yet."
"I'm not as good at this as others."	"I'm getting better with practice."
"Nothing ever seems to go right."	"I see where I made a mistake."
"I'm either good at something or not."	"I can get better with practice and feedback."
"She's better than me at everything."	"She inspires me to improve."

In the preface to our hymn book, the First Presidency referred to this principle of substitution. While written about singing hymns, the principle is still very applicable about replacing one set of thoughts or beliefs (such as fixed mindset) with a different set of thoughts or beliefs (such as growth mindset). They wrote:

> We encourage you to memorize your favorite hymns and study the scriptures that relate to them. Then, if unworthy thoughts enter your mind, sing a hymn to yourself crowding out the evil with the good.[2]

2. "First Presidency Preface," *Hymns,* ix–x.

Many of our hymns even embody a growth mindset and can be used as substitute triggers to reorient our thinking and beliefs. Here's just a few examples:

Now Let Us Rejoice (#3)
They, the Builders of the Nation (#36)
Press Forward Saints (#81)
Improve the Shining Moments (#226)
You Can Make the Pathway Bright (#228)
Put Your Shoulder to the Wheel (#252)
Let Us All Press On (#243)

Our mindsets can change and evolve. Growth mindsets expand our possibilities while fixed mindsets limit them. We broaden our mindsets when we confront our fears and develop plans for dealing with the unexpected.

Activity: What's the Worst that Could Happen

Purpose

Help family members avoid "catastrophizing" upcoming or potential events by creating a short skit that shows a range of possible ways to act and react to difficult situations.

Instructions

Pick an upcoming event or something that your children seem to be worried about. This could be anticipating a relocation to a new area or a potential job loss or having a grandparent move into the house who has an illness. Alternatively, it could be an upcoming prom or friend's birthday party or another local event.

First, describe the "scene" with some details that your children can easily relate to. Then, distribute the following set of index cards to each family member:

- What's the worst thing that could happen in this situation?
- How likely is something like this to occur?
- What could others do to make it even worse?
- What could you do that could make it better?

Second, ask each person to pass their set of cards to the person on their right. Allow 2–3 minutes for additional comments.

Next, divide family members into at least two groups. Ask each group to create a skit about the situation that you describe. Use what each person wrote on their index cards as the script as much as possible.

As skit director, tell each group that they must begin with one family starting and then others joining in later in the scene. Tell them their scene must have a beginning, some dialogue in the middle, and an ending. But how it ends is up to them!

Debriefing

Begin by acknowledging each group's performance. Allowing family members to discuss the acting first helps in later learning from the skit's message. Here's some questions to ask:

- What did you like about how it was acted out?
- What seemed realistic to you?

After giving some time and space to the performance, it's then easier to talk about what can be learned from it. In debriefing, try to focus on dealing with setbacks without becoming overwhelmed by them. Addressing setbacks without either dismissing them or becoming overly positive about them is an important part of creating a growth mindset. Here's some questions to consider:

- When things don't go as planned, what helps?
- What gets in the way of dealing with unplanned events?
- What do you feel the least comfortable dealing with if something like this were to happen?

Generalizing

Rather than "giving the answer" let your children talk and then explore options with them. Parents too often want either to give reassurances or try to smooth everything out and make things alright. Showing restraint can be difficult but allows children to discover answers for themselves that are meaningful and relevant—and most of all—lasting.

Sometimes we want to give a reason for why setbacks happen. But oftentimes we don't know ourselves and our explanations may not be convincing to us or our children. Sometimes, simply saying "we don't know why this happened" is the best approach.

Applying

But just because a setback occurred once, doesn't mean it won't happen again. Allow your children to discuss some of the worst things that have happened to them recently. Validate, don't minimize their feelings or their regrets. Then, engage in productive problem solving by discussing both prevention and intervention to minimize future setbacks.

- What is something that has happened to you in the past year that you didn't like?
- Could you have done anything to prevent it?
- Knowing what you know now, how might you have responded differently?

SUMMARY

Acting in a skit or play can help children become more expressive and better able to voice their feelings. Dressing up with a hat, coat, or scarf can both add to the fun and enhance the learning by enabling children to get outside their normal routine. It is an easy way for all of us to get outside ourselves so that we can then better assess our beliefs and actions.

Mindsets are simply our current set of beliefs. Growth and fixed mindsets represent conflicting beliefs about our capabilities. These beliefs actually interact with our abilities and help or hinder our personal and family development. When we see them for what they are, we are better able to change, learn, and grow.

#2

Losing Graciously

OVERVIEW

In today's world, leaders and others are increasingly interested in associates and friends who are able to make their way through uncertain situations by dealing with setbacks in resolving problems. The term Emotional Intelligence or Emotional Quotient (EQ) has gained popularity as a way of describing and even measuring how students, professional workers, and others are able to navigate emotionally hazardous situations and resolve problems without becoming stymied by them.

We develop our EQ at a young age by assessing and dealing with difficult situations, debriefing what happened afterwards, generalizing about related situations, and then making plans to deal proactively with similar situations in the future. Like developing our math ability or reading and grammar, our EQ is developed through practice and learning, in seeing how misreadings or misinterpretations can occur, as well as developing ways to get better answers.

How families teach and learn these EQ skills together depends a lot on the family's learning culture. Every family, group, sports team, or club has its own distinct learning culture: ways that members interact to help or hinder each other in learning, sharing, playing, and working. Family learning cultures change over time based on the ages of children, relocating or changing schools, stressful or successful experiences, and members moving into the home (like grandparents) or out of the home (like college students or missionaries). In fact, any of these events can be the basis for an activity that helps a family, and its individual members assess and improve their EQ.

Discovery learning is the single most effective way for individuals or families to develop their EQ. Its focus on providing common experiences to family members so they can assess and improve their ability to handle them is unparalleled as a learning method. It is not about giving "the answer" or asking leading questions. Rather, discovery learning helps family members see for themselves how their actions produce reactions in others and lets them use their moral agency to consider alternative ways to improve the impact they have on others.

ACTIVITY: Bidder's Dilemma (adapted from related dice games)

As described previously, discovery learning starts with a clear purpose, giving directions or setting out instructions for an activity, later debriefing it, and ends by making thoughtful generalizations. This fundamental pattern is shown in the following discovery learning activity called "Bidder's Dilemma."

PURPOSE

A useful way to teach family members how to lose gracefully is to play short games of chance that facilitate frequent winners and losers. Playing games of chance allows for an easier debrief of what it feels like to win or lose a game. Since "chance" is embedded in the game, it's sometimes easier to avoid getting caught up in the outcome.

INSTRUCTIONS

There are many different games of chance that can be used to learn and teach how to lose gracefully. In this game, each player is given 5 dice and a cup.

During each round, individual players shake and roll their dice simultaneously. After shaking, each player keeps their dice hidden under their cup so only they can see their result while ensuring their dice are hidden from other players.

The first player then makes a guess or bid about how many dice of that number may exist among all of the players in the group (for example, say, how many 5's or 2's or any other number they may select). Moving clockwise, the next player either makes a higher bid or challenges the original bidder. For example, if the original player bid "five 2's" then the next player must either make a higher bid (say, "six 2's") or challenge the original bidder. The player who begins can pick any number on the dice (but only one number) and a starting guess or "bid." Play continues clockwise with each player making a higher bid until one player chooses to challenge the previous high bidder.

Once challenged, all players reveal their dice and count the number of dice with the designated or "bid" number on their dice face. If the bid is matched or there are more dice than the last bid, then the bidder wins, and the challenger loses. Otherwise, the bidder loses if the bid exceeds the number of dice with the "bid" number. The player who loses puts aside one dice in a "discard pile."

All players start over by shaking the dice in their own cup and play continues. Each round, the player who loses puts a dice in the discard pile until one player is out of dice. At that point, the round is over.

Debriefing

In this family game, the losing player after each round is then asked the following questions:

1. What was your best move in that round?
2. What could you have done differently in that round?
3. How will losing that round make you better next time?

Play continues with as many additional rounds as the family has time to play. Ideally, several rounds should be played so that more than one family member gets asked the debrief questions and family members are better able to learn from each other.

Generalizing

While no one likes to lose, we can turn such episodes into learning moments together. The goal in talking about them immediately afterwards is to promote self-assessment and not just a "correct answer." When we "own our own feelings" and report on how we felt and then focus on what might be done differently next time, we are developing a growth mindset.

After the family plays several rounds and finishes playing the "Bidders Dilemma," they can then have a guided discussion about the game. Start with questions about the game itself and then look at "messages" that family members might share with each other. Here's some questions you might consider:

- What was something funny that happened in the game?

- What would you do differently to make it more fun if you were playing with friends?
- Were you ever discouraged during the game? What helped you bounce back?
- What's the best part about winning?
- What can you learn or get from losing?
- How can we play hard and keep losing in perspective?

Applying

Because of sports, the world is full of catchy phrases about winning and losing such as, "Winning isn't everything, it's the only thing" and "Second place is the first loser." It can make it difficult to see losing graciously as a virtue to strive for and live by. However, other catchy phrases remind us that "It's not whether you win or lose, it's how you play the game" and "Winning is more about the next game than the last one."

Statements like these can generate family discussions on personal values for daily living if the focus is on what a family has learned while playing a game and how we translate that into other school or leisure activities. We can be competitive and strive to do our best while encouraging others to do the same if we see games as fun and ways to improve our skills.

Catch phrases can be useful when looking at games and competition to see it from various angles. Here's some familiar catch phrases (you can add or modify) that can be a catalyst for applying what family members may have learned in this game to other aspects of their lives. Parents may ask each family member to say what they think about each of these statements as well as how others might react if it was the only way that we treated them.

Catchphrases:	Questions:
If it doesn't matter who wins or loses, then why do they keep score?	Will you be able to enjoy playing if you only care about the score?
You can't lose a game if you don't play it.	Is it better not to play at all if you lose?
Winners never quit and quitters never win.	How does persistence help us improve?
You are never as good as they say when you are winning, nor as bad as they say when losing.	What's the best part about winning? About losing?

You should think that "we didn't lose, we just ran out of time before winning."	How can losing help a growth mindset?

SUMMARY

Winning and losing is not just about being the most skillful. Luck plays into almost every game. The "Bidder's Dilemma" game shows how both luck and some educated guesswork matter and is fast paced enough to easily discuss the results of each round. Debriefing leads easily into a broader perspective about winning and losing graciously.

When expectations do not match an outcome or result, we typically experience disappointment. Such disappointment can be fleeting or last a very long time. If we have strong expectations about an outcome so that we feel like we "deserve" to win, it's called "arrival fallacy." When happiness is contingent on a certain outcome, changing something, or winning something, arrival fallacy is at play.

Arrival fallacy is the false belief that reaching a certain outcome creates happiness. It's the dark side of misaligned goal setting. Too often goal setting is about attaining something, rather than enjoying the process. When we focus on *outcomes—such as winning*—rather than the *process* of improving, we are setting ourselves up for disappointment. As Olympian and BYU Track coach Ed Eyestone told me while visiting with him, getting the process right and letting the results take care of themselves. Joy really is in the journey and creating that mindset is the key to winning or losing graciously.

#3

Overcoming Grudges

Life happens and people say or do things that hurt our feelings. It's almost inevitable. So, how do we respond when that happens? Ignore it? Hold a grudge? Seek revenge?

It's easier, no doubt, to talk about "turning the other cheek" than it is to actually do it. But it can be done. Perhaps the first step is to acknowledge what happened and your negative feelings about it. Don't try to sweep everything under the rug. Talking about it helps, too. But that's not always possible.

Depending on the situation, you may not be able to talk it out with the offending person or group. When possible, that is often the best approach. It lets you clear the air and leave the past behind. Let bygones be bygones. But when the offending person is either unwilling or unable to accept your point of view, then you may need to figure out other ways of dealing with your own feelings.

Most of us feel justified when holding a grudge. After all, another person did us wrong. We're just protecting ourselves by holding a grudge, so it doesn't happen again, right? Uh, maybe.

Sometimes others may mean us harm and we do need to be cautious in relating to them in the future. However, while proceeding cautiously may be helpful, resentment and making horrible a person or situation by holding a grudge isn't. Think about the effects holding a grudge has on *you:*

- Are you less willing to trust others?
- Are you irritable and bothered by other things more often?
- Do you have headaches or stomach aches from worrying about the situation?

- Are you looking for ways to "get back" at the other person somehow?
- Have you changed any routines to avoid contact with them?

Holding a grudge can cause various types of *cognitive distortions* such as *overgeneralizing*—seeing a single event or unrelated coincidences as following a certain pattern—or *magnification*—making up negative motives about someone that offended you.

The fact that holding a grudge can harm you emotionally and physically and have no effect on the person who offended you is reason enough to avoid holding a grudge. But talking about letting go isn't the same as doing it. Perhaps there is no one in scripture who could more rightfully have been justified in holding a grudge—but didn't—than Joseph who was sold into Egypt.

The story is well-known. His brothers sold him to the Midianites who eventually sold him to Potiphar in Egypt. After getting falsely accused by Potiphar's wife, he was put in prison and then three years later was released when he interpreted Pharaoh's dream. After building granaries throughout Egypt to store wheat for a forecasted famine, Joseph's brothers later traveled to Egypt to buy wheat and eventually relocated with their father Jacob to Egypt to survive the famine there.

But after Jacob died, the brothers were worried. With their father gone, would Joseph now seek revenge?

> And they sent a messenger unto Joseph saying . . . Forgive, I pray thee now, the trespass of thy brethren, and their sin; for they did evil: . . . And Joseph wept when they spake unto him. . . . And Joseph said unto them . . . Now therefore fear ye not: I will nourish you, and your little ones. And he comforted them and spake kindly to them. (Genesis 50:16–21)

Activity: Win as Much as You Can

Instructions

Form four different subgroups. It doesn't matter how many participants are in each subgroup.

Give each subgroup a tally sheet and two index cards: one marked with an "A" and the other card marked with a "B"

The objective of this activity is to "win as much as you can."

There are three primary rules:

1. You can only confer or talk with others when told it is permitted.

2. You must agree on a single choice each round: either "A" or "B". When time is called for a round, you must raise either an "A" or a "B" card.
3. Your subgroup must not reveal your choice for each round until instructed to do so.

There are 10 rounds to this exercise. During each round your subgroup will have 2 minutes to make a decision for that round.

After 2 minutes, call time, then, on the count of 3, ask each subgroup to raise their card (either an "A" or a "B").

Ask each subgroup to mark the score for that round on their tally sheet.

Rounds 2–4 repeat this process with no discussion among subgroups, even between rounds.

At the beginning of round 5, announce the following:

- You will note that all amounts won or lost this round will be multiplied by 3.
- You will have 5 minutes for each subgroup to send a representative to confer with the other subgroups.
- At the end of 5 minutes, representatives return to their subgroups and then have 2 minutes to make their choice for that round.
- As usual, after 2 minutes, ask each subgroup to raise either an "A" or a "B" card.

Round 8 is conducted like round 5 with 5 minutes for representatives from each subgroup allowed to confer but with the bonus multiplier increased to 5 times the normal value for winnings or losses.

Round ten is conducted like rounds 5 and 8 except that the payoff values are multiplied by 10.

Payoff Schedule
4 A's: Lose $1.00 each
3 A's: Win $1.00 each 1 B : Lose $3.00
2 A's: Win $ 2.00 each 2 B's: Lose $ 2.00 each
1 A : Win $3.00 3 B's: Lose $ 1.00 each
4 B's: Win $ 1.00 each

Scorecard					
	Round	Your choice (circle)	Group's pattern of choices	Payoff	Balance
	1	A B	_A _B		
	2	A B	_A _B		
	3	A B	_A _B		
	4	A B	_A _B		
Bonus Round (Payoff x3)	5	A B	_A _B		
	6	A B	_A _B		
	7	A B	_A _B		
Bonus Round (Payoff x5)	8	A B	_A _B		
	9	A B	_A _B		
Bonus Round (Payoff x10)	10	A B	_A _B		

Debriefing

In family settings, this activity can be used to talk about several types of family dynamics. Depending on how much competition or cooperation occurs between subgroups, there are a variety of ways to debrief this activity. It can be especially useful in talking about holding or giving up grudges if one or more subgroups feels slighted or exasperated.

Here's some questions that can help when debriefing:

- The objective of this exercise is to "win as much as you can." Who felt that happened?
- What dynamics of this game made it difficult or challenging?

- Did any person or subgroup do something that bothered you?
- When someone does something that bothers you and you can't really talk about it (such as constraints in this game), what can you do?
- At any time, did you feel like you wanted to "get back" at someone else because they had treated you unfairly?

Generalizing

Before subgroups are allowed to talk to each other, it is difficult to know whether to choose "A" or "B." In many instances, subgroups will choose "A" as a defensive move. When that occurs, subgroups that chose "B" may feel like subgroups that chose "A" are taking advantage of the situation. This can heighten feelings as the game progresses and turn a "risk adjusted exercise" into grievances and "fair play." At this point, it's important to help family members avoid overgeneralization or blaming. However, by allowing some of these feelings to be expressed, it is then easier to rechannel them into common situations that may occur among family members, at school, or at work. Here's some questions to consider:

- How do you typically react when you feel like you have been undermined?
- When you feel like you want to "get even," what can you do instead?
- Rather than developing a plan to get back at someone, can you acknowledge those hurt feelings and then use the situation to look at our family values and priorities?

Applying

Learning and growing is not about ignoring negative feelings, which studies show are not very effective anyway, but instead channeling them into more productive outcomes. Negative feelings like holding grudges and feeling wronged can drag us down if we let them fester, or we can "confess and forsake," which Doctrine and Covenants 58:43 reminds us is the better way, and use the path to repentance for little things as well as more significant matters.

Here's some ways to consider how parents and other family members might apply some of the things they've learned from this family activity:

1. We can only really control ourselves, not others. How can we change the "voice in our head" when we feel like we have been wronged in some way?

2. What is the best way to turn a difficult or even painful experience into a learning experience?
3. When someone says or does something hurtful, how can we avoid holding a grudge by thinking they will always do or say hurtful things?
4. Elder Marion D. Hanks, an emeritus member of the Seventy, often said that to love our neighbors doesn't require us to hug them or have them over for dinner, but instead to recognize they are also sons and daughters of God.[1] How can that perspective change things for you?
5. Seeking payback can seem like a good idea at the time, but rarely makes us feel better and often escalates animosity all around. How can we use such feelings as warning signs to avoid going down a wrong path and instead move forward by becoming a better person instead?

SUMMARY

Negative experiences can teach us valuable lessons or make us bitter, suspicious, and resentful of others. Parents often have difficulty discussing such experiences with family members because they want to press their point, which has the unintended effect of shutting down conversations rather than enabling healthy disclosure and problem-solving. Resist the temptation to give a predictable answer to a sticky problem or dismiss family members' feelings with remarks such as "You don't really mean that." Such *shaming* does more harm than good. Instead, stay in the moment with family members by listening and probing with "what" and "how" questions that promote greater exploration and more depth.

Listening isn't passive. It's dynamic. And letting family members talk doesn't mean parents only ask questions. Instead, it's all about shifting the locus of control from you as a parent to other family members. It's not about *telling* or even about *asking*, but instead it's about learning together, it's about taking a shared journey.

1. Personal interview with author, June 1970.

#4

Getting Organized

Too often parents may *expect* family members to be organized but do very little to *teach* them how to be organized. Some family members may intuitively figure out on their own how to get organized, but for most it is a learning process that must be taught, encouraged, and monitored.

At any age, children certainly don't plan to be inefficient, miss deadlines, or turn in assignments late. Yet, it happens all of the time. While some children clinically have attention deficit, research shows that lifestyle matters such as mobile phone usage or irregular routines often promote distractions and perpetuate disorganization for many of us—children and adults alike.

A major study conducted by researchers at the University of Southern California found that "in a cohort survey of 15–16 year olds . . . there was a significant association between higher frequency of modern digital use and subsequent symptoms of ADHD."[1] Further research by Dr. Jean Twenge at the University of San Diego found that teenagers who spent two hours or more on digital social media content per day were prone to higher levels of anxiety, stress, and depression than their peers as well as being significantly more distracted at school and home than their peers who spent an hour or less per day on such devices.

In addition, researchers have found that social media, mobile phones, and electronic games may make family members more anxious and less likely to follow through on work or school as well as household assignments.

1. Jean M. Twenge, "Have Smartphones Destroyed a Generation?" *The Atlantic*, Sept. 2017.

Their overuse is an impediment in getting and staying organized among adults and children.[2]

While removing barriers is important, creating positive routines and adopting new habits also requires learning a few key skills. Admiral William McRaven has written a widely popular book called *Make Your Bed* that stresses doing a few little things each day—like making your bed—which can be a springboard to take control over other parts of your world and thereby help you exert more control over other unexpected events. Having taken control over something concrete—making your bed—you are better able to tackle other personal matters and unpredicted problems.[3]

Sequencing Activity: Younger Children

Instructions

This activity focuses on sequencing, a fundamental skill in personal organization. The game involves creating a variety of different scenes with random steps and then asking family members to put the steps in a desirable sequence to produce the best outcome.

You can create your own sequencing events that fit your family's particular needs and circumstances. Here's an example for younger children and a variation to use with older family members.

Arrange and number these random steps for washing dishes in proper order:

_____ Wet the scrubber brush with soapy water
_____ Set the dishes to drain on a rack
_____ Put the stopper in the sink
_____ Wash the dishes
_____ Dry the dishes by hand
_____ Fill up the sink with warm water
_____ Squirt soap into the sink, making suds
_____ Move the dishes in the sink so there is room to soak them
_____ Rinse the dishes

2. Alexandra Samuel, "Yes Smartphones Are Destroying a Generation, But Not of Kids," *JSTOR Daily*, 8 Aug. 2017, daily.jstor.org/
3. William H. McRaven, *Make You Bed: Little Things That Can Change Your Life . . . And Maybe the World* (Grand Central Publishing, 2017).

Answer key for Washing Dishes

1. Move the dishes in the sink so there is room to soak them.
2. Put the stopper in the sink.
3. Fill up the sink with warm water.
4. Squirt soap in the sink, making suds.
5. Wet the scrubber brush with soapy water
6. Wash the dishes
7. Rinse the dishes
8. Set the dishes to drain on a rack
9. Dry the dishes by hand

Goldilocks Activity: Tweens and Teens

In the well-known fable of Goldilocks and the three bears, an important principle is highlighted. While there was plenty of porridge and enough chairs and beds to go around, not all of them worked for her. The question is not whether she needed a chair or bed or porridge, but which ones were "just right."

In this activity, a list of standard suggestions for making the most of study time are listed. That's the easy part. For each item, ask your tween/teen to give you an example of what's too much, too little, or just right in using this tool/suggestion. The task is to describe how best to use a particular idea or tool—and avoid over- or under-utilizing it. Afterwards, discuss steps for getting things "just right" in their daily routines.

	Too Little	Too Much	Just Right
Use a folder for each class			
Keep books/materials in the same spot			
Have a standard study time each day			
Begin with most difficult homework assignments first			
Have an uncluttered, well-lit place to study			
Take frequent, short breaks			
Use reminder cards/calendar for deadlines			

Create/use your own internal reward system			
Have creative desk/wall hangings and visuals			
Put mobile phone/electronics in another room			
Track actual study time			

Debriefing

Each of these age-appropriate activities:

- provide a useful and flexible to-do list
- gives family members a "say" in personalizing the list
- promotes critical thinking skills by considering alternatives

When debriefing either activity, parents can facilitate family learning the most by initially avoiding agreeing or disagreeing with family members responses (which can often just result either in arguments or stony silence among children) and instead ask them:

What might happen if you did that?

Asking this question early and often signals that you are not going to take over the discussion as a parent nor use your position to force acceptable answers. Instead, it boosts moral agency among family members and helps them dig deeper rather than merely relying on their first response. It can also help them see likely consequences or results from doing or not doing something as well.

The goal in debriefing is to go beyond a discussion by getting at the heart of a matter and ultimately applying a gospel principle in becoming a better person. Elder David A. Bednar stressed in a recent general conference that our homes are the best places for us to "organize ourselves" and "prepare every needful thing."[4] Like the temple, we teach best when we give family members experiences that allow them to reflect. As the saying goes:

I hear and I forget.
I see and I remember.
I do and I understand.

4. David A. Bednar, "Prepare to Obtain Every Needful Thing," *Ensign*, May 2109, 101–104.

Generalizing

While family expectations and rules are important, so is letting kids have some say in their personal organizing. There is a well-established principle that joint decision-making promotes joint commitment.

Words can use us just as much as we use words themselves. Consider the difference between these two questions:

"Why in the world did you do that?"
"What happened?"

The first question is accusatory while the second is neutral and is more about getting information than expecting a defense of what occurred.

In leading this discussion, it's important to *check your motive.* If you are just trying to get family members to change so that things will be easier for you, they will likely see through your intentions and will resent it and resist your "helpful" (?) suggestions. Instead, ask yourself what's in it for *them*? The more that you can see things from others' point of view, the more likely you are to create lasting solutions.

Applying

A good way to start and maintain personal organization habits among family members is to use a "Suggestions" in-basket. But rather than *giving suggestions* to others, this unique in-basket is all about *asking for help* from them. Here's how it works:

Each family member announces 2–3 personal habits they want help on from others. These could focus on certain improved study habits, or dealing more with procrastination, or creating better time management, or timely completion of family chores, etc.

Family members create a suggestions box with a headline about their goal.

Each week each person writes about something they are doing well and something not going as well for each of their goals and puts it in their own in-basket.

During the week, other family members offer congratulations or suggestions for each item.

Monthly, during a family council or discussion, family members share some of their feedback and what seems to be working best for them.

SUMMARY

Improving personal organizational skills can be challenging. It doesn't help if other family members are seen primarily as nagging or discrediting each other's efforts. When that happens, little will be accomplished from this activity. However, if children see parents as joining in and open to suggestions as well, they will be more likely to accept their own feedback. Almost like a subliminal message, a sense of "we're in this together" can spread among family members. When that happens, family members will join in willingly rather than grudgingly.

#5

Valuing Money

THE EARLY EXPERIENCES CHILDREN HAVE WITH MONEY PROFOUNDLY shapes their later ability to handle money as adults. According to a study conducted by the University of Cambridge, children as young as age 7 are capable of grasping basic financial concepts. Researchers reported that those children who are allowed to make age-appropriate financial decisions and experience saving or spending dilemmas when they are young develop "habits of the mind" that influence their attitudes toward money for the rest of their lives.[1]

But many of us are reluctant to talk to our kids about money, according to a study by T. Rowe Price. The study reports that parents typically have a couple of chances each day to talk about money with their kids as part of other activities or conversations, but they don't bring it up because they assume their children either are "not ready" or they are unsure how much to share about family finances.[2]

There is significant evidence that we develop "money scripts" at a very young age which remain with us throughout life.[3] These scripts are formed either intentionally or haphazardly based both on conversations within our

1. David Whitebread and Sue Bingham, "Habit Formation and Learning in Young Children," *The Money Advice Service,* May 2013, https://maps.org.uk/wp-content/uploads/2021/03/the-money-advice-service-habit-formation-and-learning-in-young-children-may-2013.pdf.

2. Klontz,B., Britt, S.L., Mentzer, J, and Klontz T., "Money Beliefs and Financial Behaviors: Development of the Klontz Money Script Inventory," *Journal of Financial Therapy* (2011), 2 (1).

3. "Hands On Banking K-12 Lessons," www.weareteachers.com.

family and by children observing their parents' habits. Among adults, we tend to follow what we have seen modelled by our parents when it comes to money management.

There's plenty of advice about budgets, saving, and goal-setting when it comes to teaching kids about money. Nearly all of it can be helpful if discussed and customized for your family. But the most important thing you can teach your children is how to *manage their emotions about money.* Learning good habits about saving and spending are important, but they depend upon *feelings* and *beliefs* about what is important and what trade-offs make sense to them.

Like the grasshopper and the ant—who either saved for the future or lived for the moment—we tend either toward being a "spendthrift" or a "saver" as we make decisions about what to enjoy today and what to plan for the future. Extremes can make us either overly anxious and miserly if we are constantly worried about "having enough" or we can become unprepared and out on a limb if we are short-sighted. President Gordon B Hinckley counseled that we provide "sufficient for the needs of [our families]" and while "we cannot provide against every contingency . . . we can provide against many contingencies."[4] Perhaps he is suggesting that doing our best and then being content with what we have done is the best way forward. Such contentment can be difficult to find but is worth the effort to discover.

You don't have to be an expert or set aside an hour a week to get started talking more openly about money. Almost every day you are making decisions about groceries, after school activities, household utilities and the like which you can discuss with your children. And you can do more than reiterating the oft-repeated catch phrase "money doesn't grow on trees."

Share that you have a certain amount of income, and that as parents you make decisions based on the family's needs and wants. Every decision has a "yes" and a "no" complement: doing one thing often means that you won't do something else. There are trade-offs and making choices based on your priorities matters to you.

Doctrine and Covenants 51 talks about the law of consecration in the early days of the Restoration. Because the Saints relocated so often—from New York to Kirtland to Missouri to Nauvoo—they were given specific instructions to ensure that land and property were equitably distributed, especially as new converts arrived in an area. While this law of consecration

4. Gordon B. Hinckley, "The Times in Which We Live," *Ensign*, Nov. 2001, 73.

has been adapted for our particular circumstances today, this section differentiates between needs and wants for each family:

> . . . appoint unto this people their portions, every man equal according to his family, according to his circumstances and his wants and needs. (D&C 51:3)

Understanding the differences between *needs* (essentials to maintain a healthy life) and *wants* (discretionary items that make life more enjoyable) is a good way to help younger children appreciate differences between these two concepts. In recognizing these differences, it is important to let family members voice their opinion and not tell them the answer. Focus on helping them see differences, not just have them say what you want to hear.

Activity: Wants and Needs (for younger children)

Instructions

Cut out pictures from magazines or print them from the internet with a wide range of personal and family products: clothes, food, toys, beds/blankets, backpacks, candy, school supplies, cars, boats, and the like.

Ask your children to sort them into two piles: needs (essentials to have to live) and wants (discretionary items).

After sorting, ask them to put them in their preferred order, putting those discretionary items they would like most at the top of their pile.

Debriefing

Following this prioritization, discuss the following questions:

- Which items were easy to decide on as a need or want?
- Which items were hard to decide as a need or want?
- What helped you decide where to put an item?
- How can separating needs and wants help us?

Activity: Would You Rather (for tweens and teens)

Instructions

The purpose of this activity is to consider trade-offs, delayed gratification, and opportunity costs associated with decisions that we make.

Add additional items to this list of "Would you rather" statements and print a worksheet for each family member.

Allow each person silently and individually to choose one option for each statement. Then discuss responses as a family.

WOULD YOU RATHER . . .

. . . win $1 million tomorrow or $10 million 10 years from now?

. . . earn lots of money doing a job you hate or not earn much money doing a job you love?

. . . win a two-week dream vacation or a $10,000 shopping spree at your favorite store?

. . . marry someone who is rich but with no personality or marry someone with no money who makes you laugh?

. . . spend any pocket change you get on snacks every day or not eat any snacks for a year to save for something you want?

. . . go to Disneyland once or a local amusement or outdoor park 3–4 times?

. . . go to a high-end music concert once or the movies 5–6 times?

. . . buy one name-brand pair of jeans at a high-end clothing store or several off-brand clothes at an outlet store?

. . . go on just one vacation to some distant location or take several side trips to unfamiliar places close to home?

. . . spend $500 on a hobby or on clothes?

. . . have lots of free time and no money or lots of money and no free time?

. . . get the latest cell phone or spend the same money on an outdoor hobby?

. . . eat fast food every week or at a nice restaurant once a month?

. . . buy the latest laptop right now and pay it off with interest over 5 years or save for a year to buy it outright?

. . . save a $10,000 gift for college or buy a used car?

Debriefing

There are plenty of apps and online games about planning and budgeting, spending and planning, price comparison and shopping. This exercise is about the harder questions of values and money. Like other activities, the more parents can ask instead of tell, the more actual learning will occur among family members. This is not to say parents shouldn't give their opinion. Of course they should. But timing and parental reactions make a difference in whether family members will open up or shut down when talking about money.

In debriefing, the goal is more than going over responses. It is a chance to see how family members think and feel about various ideas and options and to help them broaden their perspective. Considering trade-offs in this "Would You Rather" activity provides an opportunity for an open dialogue and a chance to consider options and opportunity costs. Here's some questions to use in debriefing:

- What 2–3 questions were the most difficult?
- What 2–3 questions were the easiest?
- What do your answers say about your preferences?
- After hearing from others, what answers might you change?

Generalizing

Studies show that most teens worry about money. A lot. More than two-thirds of teens in the country say they are stressed either about their parents' income or their own ability to make enough money when they are on their own. Simple reassurances are less helpful than open communication. Here's some discussion questions that can be helpful in a broader discussion about money:

- What does it mean to spend within your means?
- Why is debt something to be avoided whenever possible?
- What's something big that you bought that was a really smart buy?
- What's something you've bought in the past that later went on sale or a competitor came out with a better product at a lower price?
- What's your favorite family activity that you wish we would spend more time and money on?

Applying

We all know that money doesn't buy happiness but a certain amount of it is necessary to reach a level of life satisfaction. While adults at every income level say they would like to make about 15–20% more to be comfortable, studies also show that the more money people make, the less satisfied they are. Figuring out how to be content with what we have is itself an important decision in life. Interestingly, research shows that giving financially to others—such as tithes and offerings—increases our contentment and improves our mental outlook and even our physical health.[5]

The Lord gave this important promise in the Bible that has been reiterated often by modern-day prophets:

> Bring ye all the tithes into the storehouse, that there may be meat in mine house, and prove me now herewith, saith the Lord of hosts, if I will not open you the windows of heaven and pour you out a blessing, that there shall not be room enough to receive it. (Malachi 3:10)

Giving to others not only helps us feel more satisfied with what we have but also makes us more conscious of what and how we spend the money that we have.

There are dozens of financial apps and online games that families can use to assist them with additional financial planning skills. Acorns, Greenlight, goHenry, and Mint are widely used apps that help develop practical financial planning, budgeting, and saving skills for teens and tweens. The Consumer Financial Protection Bureau has dozens of online and board games that can be adapted for various ages.

Here's some ways for family members to learn real financial life lessons as they grow and mature in their financial literacy:

- Put them in charge of the household budget for a month. Give them as much latitude as possible. Allow them to determine what to buy and what to forgo based on a budget and typical expenses. Create a visible tracker on a whiteboard or review expenses and income at a weekly family council.
- Consider getting a debit card for your teens and tweens so they can budget and manage their discretionary spending and saving. This gives family members a sense of control over this aspect of their

5. Elizabeth Renter, "What Generosity Does to Your Brain and Life Expectancy," *US News and World Report,* 1, May 2015, health.usnews.com.

world, an important component of building self-esteem. Debit cards are easily available at most banks. In the digital age, learning to manage digits, not just paper money or coins, is pivotal to living in an increasingly electronic world.

- Let them earn their own money. Mowing lawns, walking dogs, and babysitting are often available for teens and tweens and teach responsibility as well as give kids money they can use to decide how to use. Consider offering extra chores they can do around the house to earn extra money as well. However, financial experts caution against paying for everything kids do or it will soon become a constant negotiation on what gets done and at what price.
- Go shopping and discuss comparison prices while doing it together. Sometimes, the least expensive items aren't necessarily the best quality just as the most expensive items may be based more on status than value. Make it fun by looking for the best deals possible.

SUMMARY

Teaching kids about money can begin at any age. It's never too early to learn. Like other things, kids learn best by experience so helping them earn money they can then save or use to buy something they want is important. Savings helps teach "delayed gratification" or the ability to resist impulsively buying or doing something simply because it is available. Such self-control comes with practice and maturity but can be improved and enhanced through the type of money management included in these examples.

#6

Becoming Good Natured

THERE IS SIGNIFICANT RESEARCH EVIDENCE TO SHOW THAT CHILDREN CAN develop a genuine sense of caring for others and a better sense of optimism about the world if they are able to do something positive for animals in the wild: like helping a baby bird or bunnies or other creatures in nature. Parents who want their children to grow into adults who value and care about others can take time to explore nature with them. It's apparent that caring about nature translates into being more hopeful about the future and more caring towards other people.

There are several popular concepts these days such as "awe walks" and "nature bathing" that promote the benefits of spending time in nature. Even when the world seems to be spinning out of control, spending time in nature can restore a sense of inner spiritual and emotional peace. The key is to appreciate the moment and really notice natural surroundings. Of course, this means setting aside mobile phones, earbuds, and other electronic gear for the time being so as not to be distracted by "unnatural things."

Spending time in nature doesn't have to involve a trip to a national park, although that can be fun and beneficial as well. Most cities have parks and green areas where you can go listen to and observe nature close at hand. But even a corner of your backyard can be sectioned off to include a nature habitat and get similar benefits as a walk in a forest or park. Let's consider the benefits of each: creating a backyard nature habitat and taking a walk in a forested area.

The most significant reward for creating a natural habitat occurs by doing something without any expectation of a direct benefit in return. That is hard to come by these days but such an important gospel principle. One way to get started is to consider ways to help honeybees, butterflies, and other pollinators by planting native flowers and vegetation that supports them. It is estimated that in some areas, pollinators have shrunk by as much as 60% in the past 25 years. Farmers rely on pollinators for many different types of crops and, even in suburban areas, designing gardens for pollinators can help control insect populations.

Nature walks are all about "being in the moment" and eliminating other distractions.

Activity: Pollinator Plants

Instructions

1. Select a location in your backyard or even on a window ledge or patio to get started.
2. Choose nectar plants that will attract adult butterflies to lay eggs for caterpillars to feed and grow.
3. Some plants will serve as both nectar and caterpillar food plants. Check with an extension agent in your area to determine which native flowering plants work best for this dual purpose.
4. You might also consider making or buying a hummingbird feeder. For the most part, hummingbirds are very picky so get one that is easy to fill and clean.
5. Keep a journal of the seeds or plants and the insects and butterflies that you see.

Debriefing

As parents, you become "nature mentors" to your kids by helping them expand their level and range of curiosity. As you ask good questions, you enable them to see and hear things they otherwise might miss.

Nature is first and foremost a sensory experience, not a cognitive one. Consequently, exploring the five senses—touch, smell, taste, hearing, and sight—while in nature. Here's some ways to heighten some of the lesser used senses by blocking out others:

- blindfold your children for 5–10 minutes and ask them to describe what they are hearing

- have them run their hands through the soil and then ask them to describe what it feels like
- use ear plugs and a blindfold, then ask them to describe anything they can smell
- take photos of plants or landscapes and use them to create a collage, then ask what was appealing to them and why it was appealing

GENERALIZING

The Lord has given us the earth to enjoy, to care for and to conserve. After placing Adam in the Garden of Eden, He instructed him "to dress it and to keep it" (Genesis 2:15) We are to be wise stewards over all that God has made.

In our day, we've been told that:

> All things which come of the earth, in the season thereof, are made for the benefit and the use of man, both to please the eye and to gladden the heart.
>
> Yea, for food and for raiment, for taste and for smell, to strengthen the body and to enliven the soul.
>
> And it pleased God that he has given all these things unto man; for unto this end were they made to be used, with judgment, not to excess, neither by extortion. (D&C 59:18–20)

We appreciate nature most when we take a step back and simply observe. Once that happens, we will surely begin to notice more and more of nature's uniqueness and can become revitalized by its wonders.

The Psalmist noted: "The earth is the Lord's, and the fulness thereof," (Psalm 24:1) which is a reminder of the importance of good stewardship as well.

We can do simple things each time we step outdoors to increase our connection with nature, get some of its invigorating benefits, and remind ourselves of the blessing we have:

- *Pause*: Take 15 seconds and step back, then ask a few sensory related questions: Do you hear any birds? Can you feel a breeze in the air? Can you smell any fresh cut grass?
- *Engage*: Pull some weeds on a fence line, skip a rick on a pond, plant some flowers and watch them grow, squat near an ant pile and check out what they are doing.
- *Ask*: Find out from others how looking into the night sky or standing on a mountain ridge provide reminders that all things testify of God (Alma 30:44)?

Applying

Spending time in nature tends to take a backseat to other activities. Yet, studies show that spending as little as two hours per week exploring the outdoors can lead to better physical and emotional health for kids. In particular, unplanned and non-directed time in nature seems, in particular, to promote better attentiveness in kids.[1] If they are not directed, they become curious and discover the world around them rather than simply passively being entertained.

Taking walks in nature—along a well-worn path or simply exploring in a park—can be easily arranged and takes little advance preparation or equipment. Just get out together! Such walks allow both parents and kids to declutter their minds and be present together.

A nature walk is not a cure-all but can be a great way for kids to unplug and become less stressed by their life indoors. Some years ago, Richard Louv emphasized this point in his well-documented book *Last Child in the Woods*. He describes a strong link between accelerated ADHD, stress, and anxiety from what he calls a "nature deficit disorder." He describes how taking a walk in a park, playing in the backyard, and sometimes even staring out a window at nature can help blunt attention deficits.[2]

A simple nature walk can help as well. Children are naturally curious and taking unstructured walks in the woods feeds this natural curiosity. In fact, research shows that such time outdoors improves their ability to learn because they are able to discover new things on their own.[3]

SUMMARY

In Genesis 1:28 we read that God gives Adam—and the rest of us—"dominion" over the earth and all things that are in it. This dominion is a sacred trust to care for plants, animals, and the earth itself in the same way that God has while creating it. God further tells Adam in this same verse to "replenish the earth," which in Hebrew means to "fill" it and not deplete it.

The Church's Children and Youth website provides a variety of activities that encourage children and youth to care for the earth, its plants and animals, with such suggested activities as the following:

---

1. Andrés R. Edwards, "Why 30 minutes of Nature a Day Is So Good for Your Health," Yes Magazine, 10 Apr. 2019, www.yesmagazine.org.
2. Richard Louv, *Last Child in the Woods: Saving Our Children from Nature-Deficit Disorder* (Algonquin Books, 2005).
3. Frances Harris, "The Nature of Learning at Forest School: Practitioners Perspectives," *Education 3-13*, Vol 45 (2), 272–291, March 2017.

- Protecting and preserving the environment
- Taking care of the world God created
- Learning to cook outdoors
- Going on a hike

Nature walks and other out-of-doors activities can be enhanced when using a camera phone to take photos. There's something about using a camera to capture an image that increases our interest and attention level. It doesn't take any particular skill other than becoming more observant—an important life skill itself.

#7

Looking Out for Others

THERE IS A POPULAR BOOK CALLED *LOOKING OUT FOR #1* BY ROBERT RINGER. Included in its message is the oft-repeated message that if you don't look out for yourself, no one else will.[1]

But what about helping each other? While we all have a primary responsibility to take care of ourselves, looking out for others benefits us all. It's like defensive driving. When we look out for others, we can help fill in unexpected gaps. And it's caring when you don't have to that makes a family, a community, a consecrated people.

Research conducted at the University of Michigan reports that empathy is on the decline among college students—more than a 30% decline in the past 10 years[2]—and a similar survey reported in Inc magazine found that empathy is the single most needed and yet underutilized skill in business today.[3] Consequently, major consulting firms like Develop Dimensions Inc (DDI) and Franklin Covey now have courses specifically designed to develop empathy among corporate managers.[4]

In the October 2020 General Conference, Sister Michelle Craig, First Counselor in the Young Women General Presidency, quotes New York Times columnist David Brooks, saying, "Many of society's great problems

1. Robert J. Ringer, *Looking Out for #1* (Fawcett Crest, 1977).
2. Diane Swanbrow, "Empathy: College Students Don't Have as Much as They Used to," *University of Michigan News,* 27 May 2010, www.news.umich.edu.
3. Justin Bariso, "Empathy: The Basic Quality Many Leaders Keep Getting Wrong," *Inc.* www.inc.com.
4. "Empathy in Business: An Unsung Resource," *Management Consulted,* 2 Dec. 2021, www.manamnetconsulted.com.

flow from people not feeling seen and known. . . . [There is a] core . . . trait that we all have to get . . . better at[, and that] is the trait of seeing each other deeply and being deeply seen."

Sister Craig then talked about her experience in developing "eyes to see." She was prompted to put away her phone while standing in a grocery store line. Looking around, she noticed an elderly gentleman in line ahead of her buying cat food.

She said something like, "I can see you have a cat," and they visited for a few moments.

Then the gentleman said softly, "You know, I haven't told anyone this, but today is my birthday." If she had not put her phone down and visited while standing in line, she would have missed the chance to wish a stranger "Happy Birthday."[5]

Malcolm Gladwell, a popular author, recently published a book called *Talking to Strangers.6* In discusses ways that we misread and misjudge people that we don't really know. It happens all the time. We make assumptions based on inexperience or even stereotypes and fail to get to know the people that we see occasionally but think we know well.

Lifeboat Activity: Practicing Empathy

Instructions

A cruise ship has just struck an iceberg, and everyone is scrambling for a lifeboat. Now, there is just one lifeboat left. It can only hold six people but there are ten people who are still on the ship. Your task is to decide who gets to go on the lifeboat. Here are the remaining passengers:

- a sailor with a broken arm
- a medical doctor who is a drug addict
- an unemployed Muslim refugee
- a farmer who owes thousands of dollars in back taxes
- an inner-city college student who has no major or life goals
- a grandmother traveling to see grandchildren she hasn't seen in years

5. "Michelle D. Craig, "Eyes to See," *Ensign*, Nov. 2020, 16.
6. Malcolm Gladwell, *Talking to Strangers: What We Should Know about the People We Don't Know* (Little, Brown, 2019).

- a salesman who supports his own and his cousin's family but often gambles away his salary
- a lawyer who defends innocent people pro bono but doesn't pay taxes
- a bitter old man just released from prison for a crime he didn't commit
- an assisted living nurse who attends church but ignores most patients
- a blind teenager
- a 75-year-old senior missionary returning home

Debriefing

This activity can help identity and potentially reshape values by forcing difficult choices. Use these questions when discussing the activity:

- What was difficult for you in making your decisions?
- What were the 2–3 considerations that were most important to you when making your choices?
- There is limited information about each passenger. What assumptions did you make to help "fill in the gaps"?
- What "blind spots" can occur when we fill in gaps too much?

As you discussed your choices as a family, what insights from others were the most helpful to you?

Generalizing

This activity becomes relevant when considering how we might approach similar real-life situations. Even at a young age, we hear and see things on the news or in the neighborhood that cause us to draw conclusions about others. Sometimes, as Sister Craig noted, we may not even "see others" at all despite passing them in the street or hallways.

Developing empathy is about letting the Lord help us so that we can "see with [our] eyes, and hear with [our] ears, and should understand with [our] hearts, and should be converted, and I should heal them" (Matthew 13:15).

There is an oft-repeated phrase about "walking a mile in another person's shoes" to see things from their point of view. While helpful, developing empathy requires seeing the world as they see it, recognizing its limitations and its opportunities.

Here's some things we can do intentionally to develop empathy:

- *Give people the benefit of the doubt:* We can assume good intentions and realize that most of the time most people are trying to do the best that they can.
- *Be curious:* The more willing we are to notice and visit with people, the more likely we are to become more aware of others and their world.
- *Lean into differences:* No two of us are exactly alike and yet all of us share so many common bonds. Recognizing differences can be an invitation to explore and discover.

Applying

A good way to begin developing empathy is to visit a food kitchen, refugee center, or language training center. However, we can implicitly feel a sense of superiority in "helping" others if we are not careful. The best way to guard against that is to really get to know 1–2 people when visiting these sites. When we individualize such visits, they become more meaningful.

Then, later in a family discussion, you might consider some of the following questions:

- Why do you think people are poor?
- What challenges do refugees have in this country?
- What makes it difficult for new converts to feel welcome at church who speak another language?

SUMMARY

During the difficult days when the Saints were expelled from Missouri by order of the governor and were gathering into Nauvoo, townspeople in Quincy, Illinois took the unusual steps to welcome these newcomers—refugees from persecution—by taking them into their homes and giving them food and shelter. There were no federal agencies coordinating this effort, no town council meetings requesting it, just good people who extended themselves to others who they did not even know.

In History of the Saints, it recorded this expression of heartfelt empathy by the citizens of Quincy, Illinois toward the Saints:

> 'We have to do something' became the hue and cry of some. Canoes were loaded and men braved the huge chunks of ice to carry supplies to the helpless. Finally in February 1839, the River froze and the saints crossed into the open arms of the citizens of Quincy. 1600 Quincyans and their neighbors out in the county

> took in more than 5000 Mormons for 4 months. They gave them food, shelter, jobs—kindness!
>
> When Joseph Smith escaped imprisonment, he found Emma in Quincy. It was May 4, 1839, at a late General Conference of the Church when Joseph rose to speak, but he could not. As he looked out over his people and their benefactors, he was so moved, that in quiet dignity, he wept![7]

Perhaps this example of kindness displayed by the citizens of Quincy is a sufficient reminder that the differences that divide us are nothing compared to the humanity that unites us.

7. "Quincy: City of Refuge," *History of the Saints,* www.historyofthesaints.org.

#8

Developing Good Manners and Avoiding Rude Behavior

There is an old saying, "Your thoughts are private, but your behavior is public." How we act tells volumes to others about who we are and how we regard them. Most of us recognize rude behavior immediately in others, but perhaps are a little less aware of it in ourselves. And maybe even when we want to change and become more respectful, we may have conflicting views on when that is applicable and when we need to "stand up for ourselves."

A recent survey reported that 65 percent of Americans see lack of civility as a "major" problem. Some examples they consistently cite of incivility and bad manners include:

- screaming at a child when irritated
- yelling or honking at other drivers on the road when cut off
- slamming a door when upset[1]

These are simple examples of rude behavior. The type that breeds poor manners and incivility. But rather than just focusing on such behavior, looking beyond what's obvious to what might be motivating such actions can better address incivility at its core. As Anthony J. D'Angelo, founder of Collegiate Empowerment, noted: "When solving problems, dig at the roots instead of just hacking at the leaves."

1. Powell Tate, "National Civility Survey," *KRC Research* (2010), www.webershandwick.com/uploads/news/files/Civility_2010_PoliticalImplications.pdf

While being polite is often equated with good manners, civility is perhaps best defined as how we regard and treat others. At times, we may all behave poorly. But perhaps, because of extenuating circumstances, we excuse ourselves. We have our reasons, and we silently justify acting the way that we do.

Everyone, even children in the same family, have a unique "backstory." We add to that backstory every day through the decisions and choices that we make. Changing that backstory means having different experiences and then choosing to interpret events in a new way. It's not about telling or even merely showing others how to act differently, it's instead experiencing and interpreting events in a new light.

The Book of Mormon tells how Alma found the fundamental "virtue of the word of God" more influential in changing what others did than focusing on their actions alone. In essence, Alma gave those he taught a different mindset—a new identity—that enabled them to see themselves and others in a new light. Good behavior then followed.

> . . . the word had a great tendency to lead the people to do that which was just—yea, it had had more powerful effect upon the minds of the people than the sword, or anything else, which had happened unto them—therefore Alma thought it was expedient that they should try the virtue of the word of God. (Alma 31:5)

Elder Boyd K. Packer emphasized this same principle by explaining, "True doctrine, understood, changes attitudes and behavior. The study of the doctrines of the gospel will improve behavior quicker than a study of behavior will improve behavior."[2] In other words, focus on who we really are and what we can become, and many unwanted daily habits will resolve themselves.

But children—at all ages—must be taught these principles. And "if the learners have not learned, then the teacher has not taught." Like most other gospel virtues, we teach best by having experiences and then drawing valid conclusions from them together. As the Ethiopian noted when Philip ask him if he understood what he was reading from the scriptures:

> And Philip ran thither to him, and heard him read the prophet Esaias, and said, Understandest thou what thou readest?
>
> And he said, How can I, except some man should guide me? And he desired Philip that he should come up and sit with him. (Acts 8:30–31)

2. Boyd K. Packer, "Little Children," *Ensign*, Nov. 1986.

Sometimes good managers and etiquette can seem old-fashioned or even irrelevant. And perhaps some Victorian practices are no longer applicable. After all, few gentlemen today would be expected to take off their coat so a lady avoids stepping in a rain puddle.

But seeing the purpose behind accepted polite practices and slowing down enough to notice when a helping hand can be extended are never out of vogue. Good manners are as much about extending ourselves to others as it is about proper etiquette.

Fundamentally, good manners have three key ingredients. Here's a short description and some possible activities for each key ingredient:

1. **Attention**—These days it's easy to tune out others by putting our nose in a phone or screen. "I Spy" is a simple game to help children notice the world around them.
2. **Taking Turns**—This skill is fundamental to civility and can be practiced with different types of age-appropriate games. "Break the Ice" and "Jenga" are both engaging and implicitly teach taking turns.

   Cooperative Storytelling is a simple activity that promotes taking turns and can be started anytime, anywhere, at a moment's notice. The rules are simple. The first person starts a story with just one sentence. Then, the next person adds a sentence consistent with the basic storyline. No one can offer suggestions for how the story goes. It can have as many rounds as you'd like to have. Generally, however, it's better to announce the length (in rounds or minutes) so that participants know what to expect.
3. **Kindness**—While most children might acknowledge that kindness is important, they may also feel that it is "overrated" in a competitive, get ahead world. Helping them identify and discuss their own "tricky situations" can occur when they are able to see the negative, perhaps even unintended consequences, of being rude or unkind.

   Paper bag storytelling is one way to help children consider the pros and cons of kindness by letting them identify possible outcomes in various scenarios. Here's how it works:

   Cut out pictures/scenes from magazines showing kindness or unkindness in action and put them in a pile.

   Ask each child to pick 2–3 scenes that they would like to be part of and 2–3 scenes they would like to avoid.

Have them put these scenes in one of two paper bags labeled either "Join In" or "Avoid."

Take turns selecting scenes from each bag and then rotating around a circle of family members who each create or make up a dialogue about what might be happening in that scene.

Have the person to the left of the storyteller comment on "What would make this situation worse?" Then, have the person on the right of the storyteller comment on "What would make this situation better?"

Debriefing

As always, it's the thoughtful and provocative questions that allow us to consider our ways and perhaps choose a different course of action. Here's a few starter questions that can be used for the activities I've just described or others that you might create on your own.

- What behavior is okay at home that's not okay at school?
- Are family members more likely to be rude to each other than to strangers?
- What do you see people doing in public that bothers you?
- Aren't good manners just being fake?
- When is texting rude?
- Does social media contribute to or detract from civility in today's world?

Generalizing

In his book *How Rude! The Teen Guide to Good Manners, Proper Behavior, and Not Grossing People Out,* noted school psychologist Alex Packer describes a variety of relatable scenarios and then asks readers to consider options when faced with these uncertain situations. He notes that:

> We can never create enough rules to anticipate every possible life situation. But we can help students create their own guidelines to assess, both before and after an action takes place, behavior that is rude and inappropriate or kind and respectful. Seeing and describing bad examples helps students embrace and apply their own general principles for politeness.[3]

3. Alex J. Packer, *How Rude! The Teen Guide to Good Manners, Proper Behavior, and Not Grossing People Out* (Free Spirit Publishing, 2014).

Applying

A way to help family members link polite and respectful actions to everyday situations is to give them specific situations and ask how they might respond. Here's an example:

> You are standing in the school hallway visiting with friends when a classmate trips and everything goes flying: books, papers, lunchbox, you name it. Initially, it seems funny. But what if it were you? What would you want others to do?
>
> There's perhaps both an obvious suggestion—help the classmate pick up their stuff—and a more nuanced course of action: laugh it off with them, minimize the embarrassment. How could you do that?

Here's some related questions to consider when discussing how to apply good manners and civility in daily life:

- Can you think of specific situations where you responded to rudeness with more of the same? What impact did it have?
- Does ignoring rudeness help it go away or encourage it?
- Can you think of examples where responding to unkindness with kindness didn't help? What about other times when it did help? What seemed to make the difference?

SUMMARY

Perhaps there is no more basic gospel doctrine than the Savior's admonition: "And as ye would that men should do to you, do ye also unto them likewise" (Luke 6:31). But reciting this principle is not enough. We must both teach and practice it. We teach best, of course, not by simply repeating the words but instead by guiding family members to discover for themselves its many benefits.

#9

Developing Empathy

EMPATHY IS WOVEN INTO THE FABRIC OF THE GOSPEL. NEARLY EVERY admonition in the scriptures on how to treat others begins with empathy. As Paul noted: "Rejoice with them that do rejoice, and weep with them that weep" (Romans 12:15). Developing empathy in family members is important because it teaches them to observe, reflect, and develop their own character and Christlike attributes.

Sometimes family members or others their age may act tough or uncaring when they are instead shy and uncertain what to say or do in stressful situations. They may want to reach out to others or offer consoling encouragement but get tongue-tied so say nothing and stay aloof.

Research at Utrecht University in the Netherlands has now shown that there are two distinct aspects of empathy and each needs to be nurtured in younger children as well as adolescents in order to be developed. These are called "cognitive empathy" and "affective empathy."[1]

Cognitive empathy can be described as the ability to mentally think about things from another person's point of view (sometimes called perspective-taking). Affective empathy, on the other hand, is the ability to recognize and respond to others' feelings appropriately. Developing each of these two types of empathy helps us with social problem-solving, managing our emotions, and avoiding unintended conflicts.

1. Caspar Lissa, et al., "The Longitudinal Interplay of Affective and Cognitive Empathy Within and Between Adolescents and Mothers," *Developmental Psychology* (December 2013), 50 (4).

DEVELOPING COGNITIVE AND AFFECTIVE EMPATHY

Research into these two types of empathy has found that girls begin to develop cognitive empathy earlier than boys with affective empathy rising throughout their teen years. However, it takes boys longer to develop cognitive empathy—perhaps due to testosterone—and social pressures may make it difficult for them to show affective empathy in group settings.[2] In other words, for both boys and girls, hormones play a part in developing and expressing empathy. It's not only a matter of learning new skills but also recognizing developmental gender differences. It's not just about learned attributes since physiology plays a part as well.

It's not always easy to find the right time or place to have a conversation that nurtures both cognitive and affective empathy with family members. Sometimes, the more informal the setting, however, the more lasting the realization. Pick and choose when to have these chats and notice what family members have to say rather than merely pushing an agenda. Teenagers seem particularly good at figuring out when others are genuinely interested in what they have to say.

Listening is an essential element in empathy, but listening is much more than being quiet while someone else is talking. It is seeking fully to understand someone else before offering your own perspective. It is recognizing the thoughts, feelings, and experiences of others even when they are not fully articulated by them.

Learning to listen with empathy can be especially challenging for family members who may have attention issues or difficulty with social skills. Picking up nonverbal cues may be particularly problematic for them. They may not notice or even recognize the sentiments that others are trying to communicate. But listening is a learned skill. Like other skills, it may come more easily for some but can be learned by anyone.

Informal Activities

Creating role-playing scenarios can be an especially helpful way in developing both cognitive and affective empathy. Again, this can be done both formally and informally. For instance, an entertaining and purposeful way to develop cognitive empathy might be to notice and imagine what passersby might be

2. Sue Shallenberger "Teens Are Still Developing Empathy Skills," *The Wall Street Journal.* 15, Oct. 2013, www.wsj.com.

saying to each other while you and other family members are out shopping or waiting on a street corner. You can stimulate such conversations with family members by asking them to guess about various passersby's background, concerns, and perspectives. Here's some "prompts" that might help:

- What was life like for them as a child?
- How did they become who they are today?
- What do you think they might hold dear?
- What would a really good day be like for them?

It can also help to discuss situations that your teenager might see in TV shows with fictional characters. Ask them if they relate to a particular person in the show and why. Then, ask them the questions cited above to stimulate their thinking and find out how they might relate to these fictional characters.

Debriefing

Based on family members' responses, you might take note of any biases, stereotypes, or negative comments based on appearances. Then, decide to probe a little more into these impressions or discuss them later. Rather than reprimanding or disagreeing with any intolerant remarks, help family members go beyond appearances and consider what they might hold dear, why they would hold it dear, and what you could learn from them.

Planned Activities

In addition to informal discussions that promote cognitive and affective empathy, role-playing activities at home can also help prepare family members in dealing with similar situations in real life.

Role-playing scenarios need to be realistic and relatable with opportunities to explore, investigate, and experiment. Short scenarios often work best and allow family members to improvise and include specifics for their personal experience and personal circumstances. Other family members who may be observers need to be supportive and provide a helpful learning environment. Here's five examples that can be adapted for individual circumstances:

Scenario 1: For no apparent reason, a friend has been really grumpy for weeks. How could you bring this up?

Scenario 2: A new boy has started school, but he sticks to himself and doesn't seem to want to make friends. What could you do?

Scenario 3: A classmate's father has just passed away and she spontaneously bursts into tears several times during the day. How might you approach her?

Scenario 4: Someone in your ward youth group has just told you that they're upset because their parents are getting a divorce. What might you do to help?

Scenario 5: A member of your class at school is an immigrant and gets very startled and jumpy whenever there is a siren. What could you do?

Debriefing

Following the role play, ask the family member to consider these

- If you were in this person's place, what would you like others to do?
- What would you not want others to do or say?
- What are some other ways you can try to understand their situation?

Generalizing

We rarely know the details of someone else's situation. Consequently, when trying to empathize, we can easily make bad assumptions or have false impressions about a situation. That doesn't mean we shouldn't try to put ourselves in someone else's shoes. Their shoes won't fit us, but we can still learn something about them.

We all have biases; it's recognizing them and doing something about them that matters. If we let our natural curiosity take over and we find out about others' unique qualities and individual circumstances, we can push past cultural stigmas and biases.

Asking questions helps unless we are seen as nosey or gossipers. Showing ourselves to others turns mere "question asking" into a conversation. It creates a dynamic two-way conversation rather than a passive activity. Here's some additional tips for engaging others and enhancing empathy:

- Lean forward slightly and maintain eye contact
- Pay close attention to others facial expressions
- Avoid interrupting
- Ask open-ended questions
- Put away your phone

Applying

Empathy includes acknowledging and even validating the experiences of others. When we brush off or dismiss others' experiences or emotions by saying such things as "Relax" or "What's the big deal?", we are not respecting them. How we respond to expressed feelings—frustrations or achievements—is central to whether the person continues to share or closes off.

When someone says things like "I'm sad," "I'm angry," or "I'm frustrated," validate it first before saying anything else. This is important. Then, ask for more details.

We enhance empathy when we focus on similarities rather than emphasizing differences among family members or groups. When we see what is common, we are better able to bridge gaps for what may not be common or shared.

SUMMARY

Empathy is about understanding other's feelings and reactions in any given situation. There are a variety of movies and books about "trading places'" that show how different environments and circumstances can change people's perspectives. Trading places with someone else for an hour or a day can be a great family activity to promote empathy. You can do this by visiting a mosque or a synagogue or even making arrangements with neighbors or friends to have a "children exchange" for a weekend. By doing chores and other regular activities at another family's house, family members can both see and experience differences that can be life changing.

#10

Replacing Envy with Generosity

Envy turns life into an endless competition that nobody wins. We may want the best for others until they seem to get something that we feel like we are missing—even if we really don't want it ourselves.

Take two sisters: Heidi and Laurie. They've always been close and even shared clothes throughout their growing up years. As she began high school, Heidi ran track and consistently improved her time at each meet, even qualifying for region her junior year. Then, in her senior year, her younger sister started high school and competed in some of the same longer distance races. Laurie consistently improved her freshman year until the two girls were both running varsity and vying to see who came in first at each meet.

In a moment of candor, here's what Heidi said about her younger sister and running:

> I always knew Laurie was going to be fast and I didn't mind it when she was in middle school, but when she was in high school and we were both competing in the same races, I got jealous. I wanted to do well my senior year and get accolades for winning races. Instead, here I was sharing the spotlight with my little sister who was faster than me. It just didn't seem fair.[1]

Ah, envy, the green-eyed monster. Wouldn't it be great if we could just shut off the voice in our head and ignore it?

But it's not that easy. Trying to force out negative feelings by ignoring them almost never works. Comparisons are inevitable, too. Whether we like it or not, before we are born we'll have our height, weight, and other factors

1. Personal interview with the author.

compared to what is normal or average or some other kind of measuring stick. In school or sports, there's someone giving us a grade or noting the score at the end of a sporting event all the time.

So, while comparisons are everywhere, how we deal with them isn't predetermined. We can see someone else's good fortune as less for us or we can look for ways for everyone to get more. It's called an "abundance mentality" rather than a "scarcity mentality."

With a scarcity mentality, if you win, then I must lose. In an abundance mentality, we can all benefit from each other and even turn competitions into "win-win." It's a fundamental mindset shift emphasized by Stephen Covey in his book *Seven Habits of Highly Effective People.*

When developing this concept, Stephen Covey visited with a small group of students and asked us to think about how we could put it into practice. In a scarcity mindset, he said, everyone wants to get "their piece of the pie." And more for you means less for me. But with an abundance mindset, the focus is on getting the pie bigger so that everyone benefits. Rather than seeing each other as competitors, we see each other as mutual benefactors.[2]

Conner Mantz from Brigham Young University and Adrian Widschutt from Florida State University showed how competitors can be colleagues and competition turned into cooperative action during the 2020 Men's National Championship Cross Country Meet. With about a kilometer left in the race, Conner was in third place and Adrian in fourth place. As a coach from another team remarked, they looked like they were out of the race.

Then, Adrian caught Conner and said, "I think we can catch those lead guys if we draft for each other." Conner hardly knew Adrian but accepted this invitation to help each other. Running close together and letting each other lead for a while, they exchanged places for some distance. Feeling energized, Conner took off. A coach from another team remarked later: "It was like Rocky getting up off the mat and taking charge."

Conner raced passed both lead runners and finished first with Adrian not far behind finishing in second place. By working together, both runners in this national championship benefited. Their "abundance mentality" allowed each of them to prosper.[3]

2. Stephen R. Covey, *The Seven Habits of Highly Effective People: Restoring the Character Ethic* (Simon and Schuster, 1989).

3. Personal interview with the author.

ACTIVITY: Mine Field

INSTRUCTIONS

1. Use masking tape to lay out an 8 x 8 foot grid with each square large enough to step into easily.
2. Tell family members there is a predetermined route that you have set up that will allow the family members to get to the other side of the grid.
3. They will need to determine the safe passage through trial and error.
4. Only one person can step into the grid at a time.
5. You have 5 minutes to plan and then there can be no additional verbal communication.
6. Once a person in the grid steps on a mine, they must retrace their steps to exit the grid and "go to the back of the line."
7. A new family member then retraces safe passage (as far as it is known) and then takes another step to search for safe passage.

One person (facilitator) sets up a route/safe passage in advance and puts it on a hand-drawn grid. This "safe passage" is the only way through the minefield. No one else sees this route; they must discover it themselves throughout this activity.

The facilitator stands at the opposite end of the maze so that they can easily determine when a family member steps on a mine and must return to the starting position outside the grid.

Make an "explosion" sound or ring a bell each time a family member steps on a mine.

DEBRIEFING

- What was this experience like for you?
- What part was hard?
- Use one word to describe how you are feeling.
- What seemed to help/hinder progress?
- When the family was really working together, what did different members do?
- When things were not going well, what did different family members do?

Generalizing

We each have our strengths. Sometimes there is a big focus on taking our strengths for granted and addressing our weaknesses or areas for improvement. Much of that kind of focus can be misplaced. Another approach is to assess our strengths and expand upon them, driving out negative thoughts and feelings.

In this activity, some family members may have done better at certain times than at other times. Some may remember previous steps; others may be more comfortable with trial and error. Seeing each other's strengths and building upon our own strengths can be difficult.

The opposite of generosity is envy. Elder Jeffrey R. Holland said:

> It has been said that envy is the one sin to which no one readily confesses, but just how widespread that tendency can be is suggested in the old Danish proverb, "If envy were a fever, all the world would be ill."[4]

Envy is downgrading the contribution of others and rationalizing our own contempt as justifiable criticism.

Because it is so hidden, envy and jealousy can be among the most destructive vices of our time. I can point out other weaknesses and extrapolate a whole raft of related shortcomings.

When we see someone who has done something better than we have done, there's at least two ways to respond:

1. Minimize their achievements and point out flaws in their actions.
2. Celebrate their skills and see how you can learn from what they've done.

An abundance mindset takes nothing away from your own abilities. It simply adds to what you already have. But it takes acknowledging that we may all have this very human tendency and, without diminishing ourselves or others, find ways to celebrate every good effort, every compassionate act, every good deed. Start by generalizing from this experience to other life experiences with these questions:

- What principles does this activity help teach us?
- Do any of you feel like you were left out or that your mistakes were penalized?

4. Jeffery R. Holland, "The Other Prodigal," *Ensign,* May 2002, 63.

- When we make mistakes, how can we learn from them rather than just feel bad about them?
- Did someone do something that helped you "get back in the game" if you checked out?

Applying

Generosity occurs when we give something that matters to us or others. Sometimes this could be a compliment, other times it might mean helping someone get their groceries to the car from the grocery store. Every act where we step outside our comfort zone and do something for others without being asked or completed develops generosity. Fill your bucket and give the abundance of others. It will refill itself.

One way to discuss and apply generosity is to read a book together such as *Fill a Bucket*.[5] While this book is oriented toward younger children, its message is broad and easily adaptable for tweens and teens. After reading the book, you might consider integrating these observations from this activity with some ideas from the book.

Here's some discussion questions to use with your family:

- What words or actions from others help fill your bucket?
- Have you seen others emptying their own or others buckets recently?
- When you feel other people's buckets, how have you seen them respond?
- So, what happened while playing minefield that might be transferred to other family or school or community situations to fill others' buckets?
- Who went out of their way unexpectedly to help someone else?
- How did you react when you stepped on a square that had already been stepped on? How did others react?
- How might you have reacted differently to fill the family's bucket?

SUMMARY

Generosity is more than something we do. It is how we think about ourselves and others. It is a mindset. It is enhanced when we celebrate others' successes and is diminished when we make comparisons and diminish ourselves. When

5. Carol McCloud, Katherine Martin, and David Messing, *Fill a Bucket: A Guide to Daily Happiness for Young Children* (Ferne Press, 2008).

we think that we must be the best or when we see others only as competitors, we are less likely to develop generosity.

Examining our feelings helps us see more clearly what we really care about—as opposed to those things we think we should care about. Acknowledging envy helps us see ourselves better—and make decisions about changing our feelings and doing things differently. Rather than comparing ourselves to them or diminishing ourselves when others succeed, we can acknowledge our own strengths as well as their strengths. This is an abundance mentality: more for everyone.

Envy is a natural human emotion; the kind that we are sent here to earth to experience and overcome. Normalize your feelings by acknowledging that we all feel envy or jealousy from time to time and rather than suppressing or even expressing these feelings, replace them with generosity: first, by celebrating others' achievements; second, acknowledging our own strengths; and third, going out of our way to do something for another person that no one else can do at that particular moment. By doing so, we develop generosity. Seize the day!

#11

Living Purposefully

WHEN YOU ARE WITH OTHERS AND THEY ARE CONSTANTLY CHECKING TEXTS, scrolling on social media, or otherwise engaged with their mobile phone, it can feel like you are not really with that person. When you are trying to have a conversation, it sends a clear message that you are playing second fiddle. The term for such inattention to people around you is called *phubbing.*

There have been many studies about teenagers and mobile phones, but perhaps a study about keeping or giving up a phone during a test is particularly relevant.

In this particular study, high school students were asked to turn off and silence their phones while performing memory tasks. Some students were allowed to keep their phone in their pocket (still turned off the entire time); while other students had them taken away and put in another room. Those who had the phone with them did significantly *worse* on the memory tasks than those whose phones were in another room. In other words, the attention and energy it takes *not to check* a phone seems to cause "brain drain."[1]

While cyberbullying gets a lot of attention, too many students face micro-emotional stress when they are left out of group chats. When this happens during the school day, it can make it very difficult to focus on schoolwork.

Studies have shown increasing rates of depression in adolescents, especially in girls, who check their phones frequently throughout the day. By contrast, other studies find that face-to-face time with friends strongly

1. Shayla Love, "Is Your Phone Actually Draining Your Brain?" *Scientific American,* 20 Dec. 2022, 62.

correlates with less depressive feelings.[2] Creating environments that promote such interpersonal interaction makes for more resilient teenagers.

There is also plenty of science to support a finding that teens may not have the same willpower or self-control as adults and may need help putting away their phones even when they want to do so. It seems that the part of the brain responsible for self-control is not fully developed until kids are in their late teens or early twenties.[3] It is the job of parents and other family members to help tweens and teens build good habits and not to overtax their self-control abilities.

Activity: Free Time Video

Purpose

The purpose of this activity is to promote positive engagement by capturing in "real time" what other students at school do with their unstructured time. It involves observing how others interact or stay by themselves at school when they are "free to choose" how they spend their time.

Instructions

Ask your kids to make short videos of their peers before/after class for several days in a row to see how they use their free time. Ask them to use the camera on their phone (or a loaner for a couple of days) to be a "behind the scenes" observer. Discuss some things to look for ahead of time as well as ways later to debrief together what they saw.

Research suggests that detailed "telling" on what your kids should film/notice and then "critique" later is largely ineffective.[4] Your kids may remain silent while you critique what they've done, but unless they've helped decide ahead of time what to look for, mostly they won't participate with you in any debriefing—or do it only superficially—and certainly they won't learn from it. However, jointly deciding ahead of time a few things to look for makes an enormous difference in later debriefing, generalizing, and applying new

2. Elizabeth Scott, "The Stress of Constantly Checking Your Phone," *Very Well Mind,* 17 Mar. 2021, www.verywellmind.com.
3. "A Teen's Brain Isn't Fully Developed Until Age 25," *Paradigm Treatment,* 23 Feb. 2021, www.paradigmtreatment.com/teens.
4. Lisa Damour, "Should You Track Your Teens Location?" *The New York Times,* 29 Aug. 2018, www.nytimes.com.

insights. What your kids see and are willing to discuss with you depends a lot on setting up the activity together.

Remind them to "pan the room" for 1–2 minutes with their camera to get a full view of "who's doing what." Rather than prod them to make certain observations, encourage them to be like a "film crew" that is simply recording a day in the life of other students. If asked what they are doing, they can simply reply they are taking random events during the day to discuss school happenings with their parents.

Debriefing

A fundamental feature of debriefing is asking *descriptive* questions about what happened and avoid *leading* or *rhetorical* questions that are really just camouflaged statements about what you think. Leading and rhetorical questions shut down discussion by communicating that you already know the answer to your question but are just waiting to see how long it takes for others to get the same answer. There's always a "hidden motive" in a rhetorical question which is often obvious to everyone else but the person asking it.

Rhetorical questions can take many forms. They enable the questioner to steer a conversation to get the answer they want or to otherwise exert control. They limit the moral agency of others and rather than promote family bonding, they keep family members on edge and defensive. Here's some examples of rhetorical questions:

- "Don't you think that . . ."
- "Wouldn't you agree with that . . ."
- "If you looked closely, wouldn't you find that . . ."
- "Are you sure about that?"
- "Why do you think . . ."

In debriefing this activity, avoid "giving the answer" or asking leading questions by exploring together what may be occurring in the short films family members have made. Here's some questions that may help you teach and debrief through descriptive questions:

- Who went out of their way to visit with someone else? What did they do?
- Who followed or didn't follow classroom rules? What impact did that have on others?
- Who stayed by themselves and didn't visit with anyone else before/after class? How come?

- What did you learn about living responsibly?

Generalizing

Ideally, we reach conclusions after gathering information, weighing it, and deciding what to do about it. The phrase "jumping to conclusions" is what occurs when the information gathering is skipped, or conclusions are reached without using an agreed upon standard.

In planned exercises like this film activity, your children may feel defensive about what some of their friends are doing. Try to avoid any "shame and blame" comments as well as leading or rhetorical questions. It's important that they share their observations. Avoid "scare tactics" and promote "*share tactics*" instead. You can do this by deciding how your family might get more information about some of the "actions and reactions" they saw in their films. Alma encourages us to "experiment with the word" which we can do in many different ways.

The goal in generalizing is to draw valid conclusions that can be used in other situations. This can be difficult. What makes something valid and not a caricature or a stereotype? The scriptures and statements of the prophets are a useful guide and can be used whenever drawing conclusions that we want to apply in our everyday lives.

The scriptures and prophetic pronouncements can free us from false conclusions and thereby help us to see as God sees, hear as He hears, and do as He does. They are the best available "resource manual" for helping us draw valid conclusions. Here are some questions that can be used in this activity:

- What did you see that seems almost universal?
- What patterns did you notice?
- What did you see that you've seen repeated elsewhere?
- What scriptures might support a conclusion that you've reached?

Applying

In commenting on changes made in the Youth and Sunday School curriculum, Mathew O. Richardson, then Second Counselor in the General Sunday School Presidency, remarked:

> Some still think "Come, Follow Me" is about boosting participation, getting people to talk. No, it's an invitation to act, to exercise agency. You can do that in many ways. A person can exercise her

> agency to listen, to share, to ask questions, to respond. All of those are ways that bring blessings for action.[5]

Parents who engage family members in addressing difficult life experiences through real-time activities increase this agency to act and the relevance of family discussions. Rich gospel discussions go beyond reciting facts or reviewing lists. As far back as 1991, President Russell M. Nelson urged us to create robust interactions with learners by enabling them to consider problematic situations and use their agency to make conscious choices about what to do and how to do it. For instance, commenting on Sabbath observance, then-Elder Nelson said:

> I plead with you to do more than passively follow lists of dos and don'ts compiled by others. Generate your own policies, and live by them.[6]

The process of deciding together what to do in difficult or problematic situations after reviewing what is taught in the scriptures strengthens everyone's resolve. We make better decisions when we have a chance to "talk out" sticky situations and then make a personal decision about what we will "go and do."

People want to improve themselves and connect together, not just for rallies or socials, but to create ties that facilitate sharing and caring. This is perhaps what is envisioned by Doctrine & Covenants 88:122:

> Appoint among yourselves a teacher, and let not all be spokesman at once; but let each one speak at a time and let all listen unto his sayings, that when all have spoken that all may be edified of all, and that every man may have an equal privilege.

SUMMARY

Learning is observing, drawing conclusions, and applying those conclusions in developing personal attributes that are detailed in the scriptures. We develop those attributes by having shared experiences which lead to shared discussions about relationships with others and the Savior.

A favorite saying of President David O. McKay was: "We sow our thoughts, and we reap our actions; we sow our actions, and we reap our

5. Tad Walch, "Shaking Up Sunday School: 'Revolution' in LDS Teaching Seeks to Activate Learners," *Church News,* 28 Sept. 2016.

6. Russell M. Nelson, "Standards of Standard-Bearers of the Lord," Brigham Young University devotional, 6 Jan. 1991, speeches.byu.edu.

habits; we sow our habits, and we reap our characters; we sow our characters, and we reap our destiny."[7]

There is an old saying that "you can lead a horse to water, but you can't make him drink" which is only partially true. A horse can be induced to drink by placing a salt lick next to the watering trough. Every rancher knows that. Simply by changing the environment—adding a new element—horses will drink, and, similarly, family members can grow and change.

7. Charles A. Hall, qtd. in *The Home Book of Quotations,* sel. Burton Stevenson (New York: Dodd, Mead & Co, 1934), 845.

#12

Rolling with the Punches

MOST OF US CAN EASILY RELATE TO THE PHRASE: ROLL WITH THE PUNCHES. It's that moment when something didn't happen the way we had hoped.

Originally, the phrase comes from boxing: it's about bobbing and weaving to avoid getting hit very hard. Nowadays, we think of it as dealing with unexpected events or things that don't go as planned. Not big natural disasters, but those micro-incursions that are, nevertheless, upsetting and disconcerting. Like the car's engine that dies and you're scrambling to find the money to get it repaired, or a project that's not going well at work, or a promotion that someone else got that you figured was yours. Stuff happens.

Kids have disappointments, too. Maybe not getting invited to a birthday party or a prom or a playdate or a sports team. Such disappointments may seem trivial to adults, but they matter to kids and not addressing them in a proactive and timely way can lead to a downward spiral from which it's much harder to recover.

The Prophet Joseph Smith had many setbacks in his life but didn't let them control either his sense of purpose or his belief in himself. He once said:

> Never get discouraged. If I were buried in the deepest pit off Nova Scotia and all the Rocky Mountains piled on top of me, I would hang on, exercise faith, keep up good courage, and I should come out on top.[1]

Developing a sense of purpose and self-confidence takes time, deliberate effort, and a little help from others.

1. John Henry Evans, *Joseph Smith: An American Prophet* (MacMillan, 1933), 9.

WHAT WOULD YOU DO IF . . .

Sometimes, the best time to talk about disappointments is not during the "heat of the moment." When a family member is feeling left out or distraught or just plain sad, they may need some alone time to process their feelings themselves. However, preparing for these moments, which will almost inevitably come, can build a foundation for them to better work through their own feelings and make decisions about going forward.

One way to help build this foundation is to brainstorm possible "heartache and heartbreak scenarios" before they ever happen (hoping, of course, they never do) and thereby enable kids to come to their own conclusions about how they might deal with them should they occur. This can be especially useful as a dinner time game so that family members can benefit from each other's comments in an informal way.

Here's some possible discussion questions. Needless to say, parents participate best when probing the initial answer their children may give and helping them consider the implications of their options rather than either giving them the answers they want to hear or asking leading questions (which is simply a thinly disguised way of giving them the answer you want).

- What would you do if you didn't get selected for the part you wanted in the school play? Would you accept another part?
- What if you dropped a fly ball in a baseball game and the winning run scored? What would you say to your teammates?
- What would you do if another kid on the street accidentally broke a favorite toy of yours? What would you say to him? What would you do next?
- What would you do if a friend was selected as class president over you? Could you still be friends?
- What would you do if others working with you on a school project didn't do their part and you got a bad grade?

AVOID CATASTROPHIZING

We all tend to "see the worst" at times. When family members resort to "disaster thinking" it can easily lead to increased anxiety, stress, and even depression.

One of the most common elements of "catastrophizing" is exaggerating the effects of something that went wrong. Rather than saying "I messed up on that project" kids may instead conclude "I never get things right.

I'm a failure." This "black and white, all or nothing" thinking can be overwhelming.

It's often easy to assume that because things are a certain way now, they will always be that way. We may find it much more difficult to imagine what it will feel like when things improve, similar to someone who's been sick for so long they don't believe they'll ever get better. This type of "*learned helplessness*" occurs when a family member comes to believe that if they didn't have control over something at some point in the past, they will never have control over it again—and shouldn't even bother to try. They give up and are displaying a fixed rather than a growth mindset.

What can compound this downward spiral is not just those negative thoughts ("Things will never get better. I'm an idiot.") but recognizing that we shouldn't be thinking like that in the first place ("Why do I always go there? What is wrong with me?"). This is something of a double whammy.

Rather than trying to coax a family member "off the ledge" with reassuring statements ("Oh, things aren't all that bad"), a better option is to "unpack" their thinking by getting specific and reviewing options together. While it may not be possible to eliminate the uncertainty and ambiguity that creates anxiety, it can at least be acknowledged.

While the goal in addressing catastrophizing is to "flip the script," it begins with first validating the family member's sentiments rather than dismissing them. There's an old saying about "label it to fix it" that is useful as well. Helping someone see for themselves that they have options increases their sense of control and allows them to see there are things they can do to get the outcomes they want in the future. Role reversal is an activity that can help.

Activity: Role Reversal

Instructions

Role reversal works best when there is a realistic situation and both you and the other family member approach it in a practical, offhanded way. Sometimes this can occur spontaneously at the dinner table—"Hey, let's try a role reversal and each of us see how we would respond"— and sometimes it can occur best "in the moment" when a child feels disappointment and begins catastrophizing.

Role reversal can help family members see their own situation more objectively and dispassionately since at that moment they are not "owning the problem" but instead letting someone else imitate their feelings and reactions.

Scenario

Ask a family member to think about a time when things went badly even when they tried hard to get a different outcome. You might even brainstorm common obstacles kids their age might encounter in trying to achieve goals in school, in sports, and the like. These could include getting B's in spelling regardless of how hard you try, not doing well in a sport because of your size, or something similar.

Pick a scenario and describe it briefly, then "reverse roles" with other family members participating in something that is not personal to them.

Debriefing

Like any other discovery learning activity, the real benefits come by debriefing, generalizing, and applying what occurred during an activity. Without making it overly ponderous, the goal is always to help family members experience something different or new that allows them to choose a different course of action. By seeing a situation in a new light, they can then choose "to act for themselves and not be acted upon" (2 Nephi 2:26).

Here are some questions that can be useful in debriefing a role reversal scenario.

- What seemed most realistic to you in this interaction?
- What happens when you get really mad at yourself? Sulk? Blame others? Blame yourself?
- What are some harmful ways of dealing with disappointment?
- What are some more helpful ways you can choose instead?

Generalizing

When dealing with disappointments, we can get overwhelmed. Stuck. Like things will never get better. At such times, rather than simply giving reassurance, look for ways to help family members "reframe" or see things from a different point of view.

One way of doing this reframing is to ask others what they did to recover when they were disappointed or embarrassed or fell short of a goal. Borrowing insights from others like this takes the pressure off and helps children see that they can recover from whatever missed opportunity occurred or reel in their tendency to catastrophize.

Ambiguity and uncertainty add fuel to disaster thinking, so look for ways to take back control of events rather than getting pushed along by them. It may not be possible to totally eliminate uncertainty, but it can be minimized—at least by our reaction, if nothing else.

Despite being a prisoner in a Nazi concertation camp, Viktor Frankl emphasized that there is one important freedom that could not be taken from him. In His book *Man's Search for Meaning*, Frankl wrote:

> Everything can be taken from a man but one thing: the last of the human freedoms—to choose one's attitude in any given set of circumstances, to choose one's own way.[2]

Worrying rarely leads to a solution. Regardless of how long you dwell on worst-case scenarios, you're no more prepared if they actually happen. Problem solving involves evaluating a situation, identifying steps to deal with it, and then putting the plan into action.

Applying

- How can you tell if you are taking things too seriously?
- What do other people sometimes say at such times that you don't like or aren't really very helpful?
- What would you like them to say or consider instead?

SUMMARY

After missing two potential game-winning field goals against a Top 10 opponent—first in regulations and then in overtime—BYU kicker Jake Oldroyd was devastated. Eventually, the Cougars won the game in the second overtime. But fans wondered: how would Jake mentally handle his two missed kicks?

The day after the game he tweeted: "Thanks everyone for the love and support. My brothers had my back last night. Next game. Next kick."[3]

Oldroyd's tweeted response reveals a crucial pattern for rolling with the punches and moving forward after a difficult outcome:

2. Viktor E. Frankl, *Man's Search for Meaning* (Beacon Press, 2014), 62.
3. Jake Oldroyd (@JakeOldroyd39), Twitter, Sept. 11, 2022, 2:59 p.m., https://twitter.com/JakeOldroyd39/status/1569068116612882432.

1. *Embrace it:* Things happen regardless of how well prepared we may be or the outcome we may visualize. "Thanks everyone . . ."
2. *Share it*: Our mindset improves when others help shoulder burdens: "My brothers had my back."
3. *Externalize it:* See a mistake as an "event" not an "attribute"; acknowledge it as something that happened but reject it as something that defines who you are. "Next game. Next kick."

Psychologists say that we tend to have a "negativity bias" to see mistakes with crystal clarity and to remind ourselves more frequently of our limitations rather than our strengths. To counteract this tendency, New York Yankees relief pitcher Adam Ottavino keeps a detailed daily journal to help him prepare for new games and learn from past experiences. The season can be a grind, he said in an interview. So, he writes down mental cues that help him anticipate situations in advance and how he will respond to them. He records successes and mistakes, good pitches and bad ones alike. Rather than mincing words, he is very direct to himself. Then, after writing down his thoughts and reactions, he moves on. He says writing things down allows him to move on.[4]

Instead of viewing your thoughts as facts, treat them as theories you're testing out. Examine and challenge them. You can do this by dividing a notebook into halves. Put difficult situations on one side and how you responded. Acknowledge goof-ups. Then, on the other half, follow it with situations that you handled well and write down what you did. Try to be as balanced as possible. Make a habit of recording a range of situations each day and what you learned from each about how to handle them productively. Through such balanced assessment you'll not only improve but also be better able to roll with the punches when disappointments occur.

4. "Why is the news always so depressing?" The Decision Lab, thedecisionlab.com/biases/negativity-bias, accessed Jan. 2023.

#13

Doing Your Best

FROM THE OUTSIDE, IT MAY BE HARD TO DETECT A FAMILY MEMBER WHO IS dealing with perfectionism. But from the inside, it may be a constant struggle for them to feel accepted, try new activities, or even see future possibilities because of a fear of failure.

A national epidemic as significant as virus-caused diseases, teen suicides are increasing at an alarming rate throughout the United States. Frighteningly, Utah's teen suicide rate is more than twice the national average based on data available for the most recent years.[1]

While it is difficult to pinpoint a single cause for this disturbing trend, researchers point to the tendency toward perfectionism and a related fear of failure as a leading cause. It's one thing to strive to improve, it's quite another to adopt the Apollo 13 mantra that "failure is not an option."

Here's some common symptoms of perfectionism among family members:

- Procrastinates starting new tasks without detailed instructions and they are 100% certain what to do.
- Gets very upset when grades or other results are less than anticipated. Takes any criticism very personally.
- Restarts tasks over and over again to "get it right."
- Fixates on neatness and appearance of work.
- Easily embarrassed.
- Believes there is only one right way to do things.

1. David Heitz, "Perfectionism," *Healthline*, 24 Dec. 2017, www.healthline.com

There is a huge difference between trying to improve and accepting nothing less than perfection in school, sports, music, or other extracurricular activities. Surrounded by constant evaluation and an overemphasis on misplaced accountability, family members can feel that nothing short of perfection is acceptable to parents or other leaders. Even the scripture "Be ye therefore perfect, even as your Father which is in heaven is perfect" (Matthew 5:48) is too often misunderstood and misapplied. President Russell M. Nelson has said "perfect" in this scripture means "complete" or whole and not flawless.[2]

President Gordon B. Hinckley often said that we can become overly concerned about trying to meet impossible standards. Instead, he emphasized that "If you do your best, it will all work out. Put your trust in God . . .. The Lord will not forsake us."[3] If we make improvement and not perfection our goal, the Lord will provide.

Addressing perfectionism starts by trying new things. Family members with perfectionist tendencies want to stay in their comfort zone and only do what is familiar to them. Breaking out of our comfort zone can be challenging at any age, but a willingness to try, to experiment, to do things that are less familiar to us increases our self-confidence and enables us to take on even more challenging tasks.

Some simple activities that promote learning at almost any age and may not be easy for a family member include the following:

- *Take something apart to see how it works*: This could include a small appliance or an electronic toy. Stoke curiosity by making it okay to "look behind the curtain" and see how something works.
- *Use the stove, follow a recipe:* Making something for the family dinner can be both satisfying and a little terrifying. The more family members learn about preparing a meal, the better they will get at it. Meal preparation is as universal as any household activity, yet it is often overlooked as a practical activity.
- *Climb a tree:* This can help children become more flexible in body and mind. It helps children think for themselves as they take risks and explore options in problem solving.

2. Russell M. Nelson, "Perfection Pending," *Ensign,* Nov. 1995.
3. "Latter-day Counsel: Excerpt from Addresses of President Gordon B. Hinckley," *Ensign,* Oct. 2000.

Activity: Hit and Switch

There are many ways to promote healthy learning, which involves trying new things, making mistakes, and doing our best. A family learning activity that does this is called "hit and switch."

Instructions

The set up for this activity is the same as volleyball. However, it can be played with a beach ball as well as a standard volleyball. Any number of players can participate.

Players start out divided equally between both sides of the net. A ball can be hit several times if needed before crossing the net.

In this game, each player hits the ball, then immediately runs under the net and joins the other team. In other words, players continually change sides until everyone is on the same side of the net. The last person who crosses under the net and joins everyone else on the same side, starts the game over again.

The object of the game is to see how many times the entire group can switch sides. If the ball hits the ground or is struck by someone who is switching sides, then play starts again from the beginning.

There are three simple rules:

1. When a player hits the ball, they must immediately switch sides
2. When a player hits the ball once, they cannot hit it again until someone else hits it.
3. If the ball hits the ground, then players return to their original sides and play starts again from the beginning.

Debriefing

This activity promotes doing your best because it is cooperative and is based on effort rather than perfection. At the end, the question "Who won?" is irrelevant since membership of each team is fluid, which also helps everyone to work together.

Here's some questions to ask when debriefing:

- What helped you to try even when you were unsure if you would succeed?

- How did a common goal—get everyone on the same side—help you when playing the game?
- How do things change when instead of "winners and losers" there are just "players and teammates" in a game?
- What did others say or do that encouraged you to keep trying even when you didn't hit the ball very well?
- What helped you do your best? How can you apply that at other times?

Generalizing

Family members can set impossibly high goals for themselves and then become frustrated when they fail to live up to them. Playing games can be more than fun, recreational events; they can also be learning activities if observations are discussed and applied.

The desire to improve can be a double-edged sword if family members become fixated with becoming the best at everything they do. Finding the right balance between doing our best and avoiding perfectionism is important for everyone.

In doing our best, we can begin by avoiding "the tyranny of shoulds." Instead of family members telling themselves they "should" do better or they "should" work harder, we can all just stop "shoulding" on ourselves!

This doesn't mean giving excuses for poor performance. Rather, it means turning off the critical voice in our heads by focusing more on *describing* what happened in an assignment or activity rather than evaluating what we did, which can promote a sense of never being good enough.

Consequently, here's some questions that can help family members discover new ways to think about *doing their best* rather than *needing to be the best.*

- Even when doing something carefully, do you often feel that it's not quite right?
- Does it take you longer than most to do things right?
- Do you feel that parents or others will think less of you if you make a mistake?
- Do you feel that your parents or others have high expectations for your future to which you might not measure up?
- What do you do when you feel like you can't be the best at something?

Applying

It's hard not to declare our performance as good or bad, acceptable or unacceptable, winning or losing. But describing what happened actually gives us a more accurate picture of events or activities without fogging them up with evaluative assessments.

The more we can be "quick to observe" (Mormon 1:1) as the prophet Mormon was even as a child, the better we will be able to give our best in all circumstances: school, work, home. As we observe, we are better able to describe what may have happened without inserting diminishing, evaluative phrases that obscure actual facts.

This helps children tame the inner critic they may have about living the gospel completely. Committing sin and making mistakes are not the same thing. Too often they are confused by children and even adults.

A sin is not a mistake. A sin is a deliberate choice to do something wrong. A mistake is giving our best effort but missing or overlooking some crucial element of an activity or assignment. A sin is intentional, a mistake is unforeseen. Both can be corrected, but they start and end in different places. We must "confess and forsake" our sins (D&C 58:43) but we don't want to confuse sins with mistakes.

While none of us really like to make mistakes, they are the best way to learn. The more mistakes we make, the more likely we are to learn and grow from them—if we take the time to observe and apply in our daily lives what we have learned. Here's some ways to help us do that:

- *Don't say sorry for mistakes*: Saying sorry implies we did something wrong. Mistakes are not about "shame and blame" but about "seeing and believing." When we *see* how we overlooked something and believe we can do better, then we learn from our mistakes.
- *Reframe errors:* Instead of evaluating ourselves and viewing errors negatively, instead become a detective and search for overlooked details. What would Sherlock Holmes do? How is this a puzzle whose pattern needs clarifying?
- *Take a step back and make future "go forward" plans*: Doing your best is all about the future, not the past. Once a family member identifies things that have been overlooked in a past homework assignment, sporting event, or other activity, put into practice what has been learned. Talk to others who can help with this process and be a sound board.

SUMMARY

When kids receive praise and encouragement, they often strive to do more and be better. But how we give praise matters. The best way to praise is to help kids recognize what they did well themselves and then further help them assess what they might do better. Instead of giving external rewards and unwarranted praise—which can include telling a child they did well even when they feel that is not the case—help them switch on their own "internal generators" by asking questions like these:

- Even though everything may have not gone perfectly, what did you feel good about?
- Where do you think you could improve next time?
- Who do you think you helped?
- What's the best part of the activity?

Regardless of their age, children can assess how well they did on a task and thereby increase their own ability to observe, generalize, and apply what they may have learned from it.

#14

Overcoming Pessimism

PROBLEMS ABOUND. IT'S EASY TO LOOK AT WORLD EVENTS AND BECOME pessimistic about the future. You may see events in your neighborhood the same way. Sometimes, bad news travels much faster and is more visible than good news. Yet, prophets have counseled us to approach the future optimistically.

President Gordon B. Hinckley devoted an entire chapter in his book *Standing for Something* to optimism[1] and President Nelson and others have emphasized the same message. However, events at school, home, or in extracurricular activities may conspire to make younger children, tweens, and teens especially vulnerable to pessimistic thinking. What's to be done?

First of all, pessimism is not an inherent trait. It is a learned thought pattern. It can be unlearned, as Martin Seligman writes in his book *Learned Optimism*. He emphasizes that pessimism doesn't really work very well in the base cases and is characterized by any of these four types of remarks:

Permanence: "Bad stuff always happens to me."
Pervasive: "Nothing ever goes right for me."
Personal: "Why does this always happen to me?"
Powerlessness: "This is impossible. What can anyone do?"[2]

Rather than merely confront these negative generalizations—which may cause kids to say them *less* but internalize them *more*—engage discovery

1. Gordon B. Hinckley, *Standing for Something: 10 Neglected Virtues That Will Heal Our Hearts and Homes* (Times Books, 2000), 115.
2. Martin E. P. Seligman, *Learned Optimism: How to Change Your Mind and Your Life* (Vintage Books, 2006).

learning so that family members can see for themselves that these generalizations are often incomplete and inaccurate.

Too often parents want to convince their children that such negative thinking isn't right, but children have a different set of experiences and may discount what others say about their pessimistic thinking patterns. Consequently, giving them a new set of experiences can be useful in helping them discover for themselves that such pessimism is fruitless and leads to a downward spiral of even worse outcomes. The starting point is an updated set of experiences.

While discovery learning methods cannot guarantee outcomes—by design they provide options and different possibilities—the debriefing discussion that follows a game or simulation or similar activity provides a real experience that can then get dissected and better ways of approaching a particular problem considered and highlighted. Through skillful facilitation, heavy handed "shoulds" from parents can be replaced with family members seeing for themselves the benefits of optimism and continually looking for better ways of doing things.

Activity: Human Knot

Instructions

For this activity, you need an even number of people from 4–20. Consequently, one parent may need to be an observer/facilitator and not a participant in order to ensure there is an even number of participants in the activity.

To get started, each person stands in a circle, looking inward, and grabs a hand from two different people across from them. Sometimes, this activity is called "the human knot" because family members are beginning with a tangled knot. Then, family members try to untangle themselves *without letting go of anyone's hand.*

The goal is to end up in a circle with no one's hands crossed in the middle. As the family members untangle themselves, some of them will wind up facing the inside of the circle and others will face the outside.

Smaller numbers of family members will be able to untangle themselves within minutes. However, larger numbers will find this activity much more challenging and, in some cases, will not be able to untangle themselves. After a few minutes, if family members are not able to untangle themselves, ask them to let go of each other's hands and start again by grasping different family members' hands if possible.

Debriefing

Successfully completing this activity requires that family members listen to each other's ideas and experiment with ways to untangle themselves. Problem solving occurs best when doing an activity and this one is both easy to set up and fun to do together. Here's some questions to help with the initial debrief:

- Did it initially seem impossible to untangle yourselves?
- What helped overcome your initial pessimism?
- What happened when you tried something, and it didn't really work?
- Did anyone seem like they were not trying to untangle the knot? How did that affect you?

Generalizing

Teachers have the advantage of "social distance" over parents who have a much more comprehensive role. Teachers do not share the same family dynamics as parents and siblings. For instance, a neighbor may be able to help your children learn to ride a bike easier than you as a parent because their tips and advice are more readily accepted as suggestions than yours which may be interpreted only as criticism. Teenagers, especially, may see parents' suggestions as personal slights. Teens may see their parents as overly anxious about drugs, crime, success, and other expectations to the point where they may find it difficult to have meaningful conversations without feeling judged.

"There's just so much more emotional weight that goes into teaching your own kids." says Dr. Vasco Lopes, school psychologist and Columbia University professor. This unique aspect is important characteristic of teaching at home. Family members never really ignore their relationships with each other even when generalizing from such family discussions as the human knot.

Research suggests that when parents' conversations at home are focused only on "the answers" that children either stop asking questions or dismiss their parents' answers altogether because they are seen as the same old stuff.[3] For these reasons, among others, it is important to avoid asking leading or rhetorical questions where it is obvious what answer is expected. Instead, ask realistic questions based on the experience the family had together such as the following:

- What did you learn from this activity?
- How does being optimistic/pessimistic help/hurt our problem solving?
- When stuck, what helps you back up and look at other options?
- How does experimenting (trying new approaches) help in problem-solving?
- How does worrying about any final outcome affect our ability to try different options?

SUMMARY

Repeated patterns of unrealistic negative thinking are called cognitive distortions. Children affected by this tendency can come to feel like the world is against them and that they will never measure up. Another example is "all or nothing thinking" that includes a child believing that if they don't get perfect grades, they are a huge disappointment to their parents and not worthy of their love.

Experiences among family members solving problems together like the "human knot activity" can reframe their thinking. Reframing is all about looking at things from a different point of view. Rather than telling children what they *should* think or what point of view they should adopt, discovery learning enables them to have a *shared experience* and debrief it together so that they develop more productive and optimistic ways of solving problems and facing the future together.

Optimists can be overly cheery and exhibit what is called "toxic positivity:" a reluctance to accept failings and suppress disappointments. Pessimists, on the other hand, can get caught up in a down spiral of worry, anxiety, and gloom.

Research has shown that mistaken expectations from either optimists or pessimists reduce personal well-being.[4] A better approach happens when

3. Whitney Goodman, *Toxic Positivity: Keeping It Real In a World Obsessed with Being Happy* (NY: TarcherPerigee, 2022).
4. David de Meza, "Neither an Optimist Nor a Pessimist Be: Mistaken Expectations Lower Well-Being," *Pers Soc Psychol Bulletin*, Apr. 2021; 47 (4):540–550.

both youth and adults are willing to test their personal beliefs, experiment, and realistically adjust their mindset and perceptions based on debriefing their own lived experiences: whether occurring in a simulation or in day-to-day living. This more realistic approach embedded in discovery learning: explore—try—assess—reflect—apply—both enhances well-being and enriches personal attributes.

#15

Appreciating Gospel Art and Sacred Music

PERSONAL DEVELOPMENT HAS MANY DIFFERENT APPROACHES AND ADVOcates on how best to rear children who become creative and responsible adults. Most advocates, however, would agree that personal development is less about "filling a bucket" with facts and figures and more about expanding minds and hearts, about how children learn to see and hear things that might otherwise go unnoticed. As Isaiah noted: "Seeing many things, but thou observest not; opening the ears, but he heareth not" (Isaiah 42:20).

Being aware of how art and music expand how we see and hear opens new ways of approaching the world for families regardless of their artistic talent or musical ability. It's not about becoming artists or musicians (although some family members may do that), but instead about being able to "see with their eyes, and hear with their ears, and should understand with their heart, and should be converted" (Matthew 13:15). The objective of all gospel instruction is not mere compliance, but conversion.

Art and music can powerfully affect our emotions. But can it do more? Can it change how we see the world? How we see ourselves?

In the preface to the Hymn book, the First Presidency wrote this important message:

> Music has boundless powers for moving families toward greater spirituality and devotion to the gospel. . . . Ours is a hymnbook for the home as well as for the meetinghouse.
>
> . . . Hymns can lift our spirits, give us courage, and move us to righteous action. They can fill our souls with heavenly thoughts and bring us a spirit of peace.

> Hymns can also help us withstand the temptations of the adversary. We encourage you to memorize your favorite hymns and study the scriptures that relate to them. Then, if unworthy thoughts enter your mind, sing a hymn to yourself, crowding out the evil with the good.[1]

Singing has always been a part of how we worship our Heavenly Father and our Savior. Singing sacred music prepares us to meet the challenges of the day. While gathered together with His disciples and prior to going to Galilee, the Savior prepared for the work of the ministry by singing together. "And when they had sung a hymn, they went out into the mount of Olives" (Matthew 26:30).

Sacred music not only helps us feel the Spirit but also enhances our ability to see ourselves and others in a new light. Gospel art can do this same thing.

On her blog, artist Samantha Kaplan writes:

> Art introduces us to a whole new set of experiences and ideas that we may have never witnessed before. These experiences allow us to look within because as people, we decide what we're seeing and feeling based on the emotional connection that we have with that work of art.[2]

Scientists say that the normal human eye actually sees many different shades of color but because we don't have the words to describe these different shades easily, we don't recognize them. Consequently, all we notice is an "average" color such as red or blue despite our eye recognizing more subtle shades such as reddish orange or bluish green.[3]

This connection between our mind and our eye is important not only in art but also in our gospel understanding. It's having "eyes to see and ears to hear" that broadens or limits our view of the world and our place in it. Works of art can broaden our worldview if we take the time to notice, describe, and reflect.

Like other skills, these perceptual skills can be improved through practice. It's not about enhancing our ability to see technical details in artwork but increasing our ability to see and then describe what we are seeing. This both increases our appreciation for artworks and transforms our thinking. The more we focus on what we see in artwork and then try our best to

---

1. "First Presidency Preface," *Hymns*, ix–x.
2. Samantha Kaplan, "How Art Can Improve Your Quality of Life, *Samantha Kaplan Art*, accessed Nov. 2022, https://www.samanthakaplanart.com.
3. Carl Jennings, "All the Colors We Cannot See," *The Startup*, 24 Jun. 2019, medium.com/swlh/all-the-colors-we-cannot-see.

describe it in unique and personal ways, the more we appreciate it and can use it to increase our gospel understanding.

ACTIVITY: Hidden Messages

The purpose of this activity if to become more familiar with the Gospel Art and Hymn books. There is a wide variety of options that can be used to accomplish this objective. For instance, family members can be asked to find 3–5 paintings or songs in Gospel Art or the Hymn book and simply explain why they are appealing to them. Another option is to pick a theme or message and ask family members to pick paintings or hymns that best represent that message and write the painting or hymn named on a piece of paper. Afterwards, much like the game Apples to Apples, each painting or hymn can be sorted anonymously by theme and family members vote on the painting or hymn that best captures the essence of that message. The goal, like other variations, is to discuss the painting or hymn and not merely select the best fit.

Here's another option: like a scavenger hunt, family members are given a list of 5–6 topics or phrases embedded in the Hymn book and asked to find them (or, with a little adaptation using "implied messages" rather than actual phrases, this can also be done with the Gospel Art book).

Here are some "hidden phrases" that could be used as a Hymn book "scavenger hunt" along with their hymn title, for reference (in parentheses):

1. "All my fond hopes are centered in thee" (Hymn 34, "O Ye Mountains High")
2. "So from the beginning the fight we were winning" (Hymn 93, "Prayer of Thanksgiving")
3. "Where in my need to know, where can I run?" (Hymn 129, "Where Can I Turn for Peace?")
4. "Standing for truth with fervent accord, teaching his holy word" (Hymn 264, "Hark, All Ye Nations)
5. "All the earth's a garden sweet, making life a bliss complete" (Hymn 294, "Love at Home")

Any of these activities can help family members explore the Gospel Art or Hymn book. These discussion questions can also help family members share their own thoughts about visual messages or sacred hymns and have them become not only used but also incorporated into family members daily thoughts and actions.

Gospel Art Discussion Questions:

- What painting in the Gospel Art book most appeals to you?
- Describe the mood that it puts you in? How does it make you feel?
- How would you describe this scene/painting to someone who has never seen it before?
- If you could add something to this painting/scene, what would you add?
- What sound effects would you add to it to make it even more dramatic and powerful?
- What do you imagine might have occurred just before this scene? Give as many details as possible.

Sacred Music Discussion Questions:

- What is your favorite hymn or Primary song?
- What makes it so appealing to you?
- How do the lyrics of this song or hymn draw you closer to Heavenly Father and His Son?
- How would you describe the way this song/hymn makes you feel in a single word (hope, awe, gratitude, compassion, etc.)?
- What drawing or painting or other image around the house evokes these same feelings?

Debriefing

While appreciating art and music can be very personal, discussing our perceptions and feelings with others helps us clarify our feelings and fills gaps by getting others' perspectives. There's no "safer" or better place to do that than in a home setting. At home, we can explore our feelings with less fear of criticism or judgment. We can both share and gain insights that might not occur elsewhere.

Appreciating art and music requires us to exercise our imagination. It transforms how we might see things into a different realm. Alma suggested how we might do this by "fast forwarding" ourselves as if we were in the presence of our Heavenly Father.

> I say unto you, can you imagine to yourselves that ye hear the voice of the Lord, saying unto you, in that day: Come unto me ye blessed,

for behold, your works have been the works of righteousness upon the face of the earth? (Alma 5:16)

Imagination can be the way in and out of any emotion. It can propel us to increased spirituality or drag us down into "doom and gloom." Exercising our imagination through art and music can help us better understand our world and our Father in Heaven's plan for us. As Alma suggested, if we can imagine being in God's presence, that can help us as we strive to put our "imagination" into practice.

Here's some questions to consider in using art and music to promote gospel understanding:

- What helped you imagine different scenes while looking at pictures in the Gospel Art book?
- What helps you generally to "suspend judgment" and imagine situations more easily?
- What gets in the way of your imagination or reduces your ability to overcome "imagination blocks"?
- What did other family members see in a picture or feel in a song that you might incorporate?

Generalizing

We can unpack or generalize learning about appreciating art and music simply by discussing what we saw, felt, and imagined. This helps us to take what we experienced in a home-based family discussion and transfer it to other situations outside the home. Sometimes, family members may diverge in how they think, feel, and imagine and bringing them "back together" through a shared conversation not only shares learnings in the family but also promotes family unity.

In order to appreciate art and music, family members need to grapple with attributes and examples. By naming, sorting, and imagining, we are able to interpret other events and activities better and thereby reduce misconceptions in other aspects of everyday life. Here's some additional questions that can help in practicing those skills:

- What did others notice in a picture that you didn't see until they described it?
- How did trying to put into words what you felt or saw help you "see more" or "feel deeper"?

- How can you benefit from seeing and noticing more in other ways at school or home?

Applying

While knowing the gospel is important, staying on the covenant path is all about living the gospel. *Knowing* and *doing* go together. The connections that we make between very different things not only broadens our world-view but also increases our gospel understanding and living. Here's some family discussion questions that can help family members make a variety of connections between appreciating art and music and turning observations and feelings into everyday living:

- What connections can you make between the thoughts and feelings you had when viewing a Gospel Art painting or hearing sacred music and your everyday life?
- How can other works of art or music influence ways in which you strive to live the gospel?
- What popular singer or performers would you like to see take a hymn or Primary song and turn it into a song? How do you think they might interpret it?

SUMMARY

The Church's Children and Youth website contains additional suggestions on exploring art and sacred music.[4]

For some, taking a fresh approach to art and music can seem daunting or perhaps not worthwhile. There is an inner critic that lives inside our heads that can dissuade us even from trying new things. This inner critic can tell us things that are both true and false, give us perspectives that can be helpful or demeaning, enlighten or diminish us.

While in mortality, it is important to distinguish between this inner critic and the influence of the Holy Ghost since "by the power of the Holy Ghost ye may know the truth of all things" (Moroni 10:5). Even about ourselves.

The inner critic in our heads is so often very judgmental and can prevent us from experimenting with new ideas or concepts. We extinguish this

4. See www.churchofjesuschrist.org/youth/childrenandyouth/youth?lang=eng

inner critic by amplifying the Holy Ghost who can bring past successes to our remembrance and drown out the sound of our inner critic.

It is much easier to replace this inner critic than attempting only to silence it. This can be done by replacing uncertainty with personal examples that refute the inner critic. We do this by reminding ourselves of concrete examples when we were successful, competent, and overcame some difficulty. Instead of arguing with your inner critic, dismissing it by recalling and mentally rehearsing past "success stories" from your own experience.

Art and music can give us fresh perspectives. They can help us see and feel differently, worthier, holier. But it takes some effort to reorient ourselves to such a new or different way of thinking. But the rewards here and now as well as in the eternities are worth it.

#16

Avoiding Comparisons

A PHRASE FAMOUSLY ATTRIBUTED TO OSCAR WILDE IS "BE YOURSELF; everyone else is already taken." There's an oft repeated saying that "comparisons are the thief of joy." And when helping others avoid comparisons, truly "more is caught than taught." What family members see and discover for themselves is much more significant than what they hear from parents or teachers.

Technology can help or hinder what may happen in the home and at church as family members either resist or succumb to comparisons. On social media, "highlight reels" from others can be clipped, edited, and promoted so they only look their very best. Never mind the daily grind or shortfalls that are rarely presented or glossed over.

Comparisons can erroneously tell us that what we can do will never be good enough. It says others are smarter, faster, better in every way than we are, and we will never measure up or be good enough. Comparisons are deceptive and debilitating. And nearly always incomplete.

Rather than simply talking about judgmental comparisons, discovery learning reminds us to look deeply at an experience and then explore as a family what we've noticed, seen, and learned.

ACTIVITY: Mask Making

This activity is adapted from Penn State University's Medical School student/faculty orientation session. Each year new students jointly create and then discuss masks about who they are and external comparisons that influence them. Here's how it can be adapted as a family activity.

Instructions

Tell family members that you are going to discuss the masks that we and other people sometimes wear. You might use excerpts from Elder Quentin L. Cook's Conference talk "Act Well Your Part" (October 2013 General Conference).

Give each family member a paper plate and ask them to draw a mouth, nose, and eyes on it.

Mention that Abraham Lincoln once said that our faces reflect the lives that we have lived: our joys, fears, tragedies, and triumphs.

Tell family members this activity is about drawing or representing some of the current influences in our lives. These include:

- *Tears*: What makes us sad?
- *Jeers*: What are social pressures and negative influences that affect us?
- *Cheers*: What personal character traits (not achievements) can we celebrate about ourselves?

Set a timer for 5–7 minutes and let each family member draw or represent as imaginatively as possible their paper plate "face" with symbols, images, illustrations, or even pasting photos from magazines (which might be available to cut up, if needed, for prompts).

Debriefing

This imaginative activity can be a useful way to assess submerged feelings or pressures that family members may be experiencing. It can also be a really helpful way for family members to see ways they can help and support each other.

Begin debriefing this activity by asking each family member to briefly describe only their *tears: what makes them sad*. Do this one by one among family members without either critiquing or analyzing their responses but ask clarifying questions that allow them to further explain what they included.

Then, look for what are common items included among *tears* before going on to the next item. Ask family members to comment on what is common and what is unique on this aspect only of the family's faces so far.

Pick someone else in the family to begin the next round by asking each family member one-by-one to share what they had on their paper plate faces for *jeers: social pressure and other negative influences.* As each family member shares their images, symbols, and drawings, ask questions that help them tell more but avoid questions that are too probing or invasive. Once everyone has explained this part of their "face," look again for commonalities and ask family members to say what they see as similarities and uniqueness about what family members have constructed.

Complete the identification and initial discussion cycle by picking a new family member to start and then describe their *cheers*: *what is notable and cause for celebration about each family member!*

Generalizing

How we extrapolate from past experiences in considering what we might do in similar future situations enhances our ability "to act for ourselves" and not be "acted upon" (2 Nephi 2:26).

When something has happened in the past that causes us to be fearful, tearful, or mournful, we are unlikely to change our point of view unless we have different experiences that enable us to draw different conclusions. Mostly, family members won't be "talked out of" their doubts, concerns, or misgivings, but they can *experience* something new or different and then *decide for themselves* to adopt a new or different way of thinking.

This experience of drawing or illustrating tears, jeers, and cheers can be a starting point for minimizing comparisons and ameliorating external pressures while celebrating our own, unique personal attributes. However, parents and older family members need to resist telling other family members what they should or should not think or feel. Instead, a more effective approach is to help each family member see for themselves when they are overgeneralizing from a past occurrence.

After debriefing, family members can then discuss together what factors may be influencing their tears, jeers, and cheers. We learn best from each other when discussing shared experiences. In this way, we can "borrow" insight and perspective from each other.

Tears:

- What have others done when faced with similar situations?
- What examples from the scriptures or literature can help inform your perspective?

Jeers:

- What may be unfounded and what may be realistic?
- What's the worst thing that could happen? How likely is that?
- What can you do in advance to minimize or prevent it from happening to you?

Cheers:

- How can you learn more about these positive attributes?
- How can you leverage them as personal strengths?

Applying

We can intentionally decide to put into practice what was learned from a past experience by thinking about similar situations.

Here's some ways to help family members put into perspective their tears, jeers, and even cheers:

Tears*:*

- Is there something that you can do about this, even in a small way? Taking action in some way often reduces our feelings of insecurity.
- How can you recognize "triggers" and give them their due without letting them become overwhelming?

Jeers*:*

- How can you learn more about what is affecting you? Knowing more increases our ability to influence the effects of social pressures or external influences.

Cheers:

- How can you visualize using this personal attribute in various situations at home, school, or work?

SUMMARY

We all make comparisons: he's taller than me, her hair is longer than mine, they have lived in more places than we have lived. As children grow, they become more aware of differences and can emotionally "load up" on the comparisons they make and turn them into extreme value judgments of worth: he's better than me, she's so pretty and popular, they have the "Midas touch" with everything they do.

While some comparisons are simply descriptive and harmless, those that are "worth-oriented" judgments are both destructive and incomplete.

We are all of "great worth" (D&C 18:10) and simply have different talents and abilities. Rather than decry differences, they can instead be celebrated. How boring if we were all the same!

It is our individuality that is of such great worth. While comparisons may be inevitable, contrasting such comparisons with your tweens and teens own unique gifts may be helpful.

There is an old fable which George Reavis has developed into a short, illustrated book called *The Animal School* that describes the dangers of comparisons and the value of individual strengths. In the book, a standardized curriculum is created for all of the animals. Regardless of their natural abilities, each animal is expected to learn to run, swim, fly, burrow, and climb. Then, a contest is organized to determine who is best. Of course, animals with wings do well flying but fail at swimming or burrowing. Animals that can swim don't do very well running or burrowing. At the end of the book, the author asks the questions: Is there a moral to this story?[1]

How would children and youth answer this question in their own families? Participating in this mask making activity and discussing this fable can help your family members identify their strengths and celebrate their individuality.

1. George H. Reavis, *The Animal School: The Administration of the School Curriculum with References to Individual Differences* (Peterborough, NH: Crystal Springs Books, 1999).

#17

Creating a Helping Attitude

> Give, and it shall be given unto you; good measure, pressed down, shaken together, and running over, shall men give into your bosom. For the same measure that ye mete withal it shall be measured to you again. (Luke 6:38)

Helping others can create a sense of belonging better than almost anything else. Helping other family members creates bonds and commitments to each other, forming the glue that holds families together. Scientific studies show that helping others also increases our own sense of happiness while boosting our self-confidence.[1]

From small acts, such as giving a smile, offering up a seat, helping with grocery bags, or extending a handshake, there are many ways to go out of our way to give to others. And when we do, not only the recipient but others who are watching such acts are more likely to "pass it on." This ripple effect amplifies such simple acts of giving to others and can have a profound effect.

Some family members seem to come with a helping attitude while others grudgingly resist it. "Let someone else do it," seems to be their motto. Some differences may be innate. But regardless of where family members are on the "helping scale," attentiveness and unselfishness can be learned.

"One definition of selfishness is 'clinging to your own comfort, advantage, or position at the expense of others.'"[2] In other words, our ability to

1. "How Helping Others Helps You", Mental Health America, www.mhanational.org/help-others, accessed Jan. 2023.
2. "Selfishness," *Family Home Evening Resource Book* (The Church of Jesus Christ of Latter-day Saints, 1983), churchofjesuschrist.org.

get outside our own thoughts and typical reaction to events is the root of either helping or ignoring others. Can we see things from others' point of view? Can we notice situations where getting outside our own comfort zone may make a difference to someone else? Do we see such situations as worth our efforts?

The Doctrine and Covenants emphasizes that we should "teach one another . . . and let every man esteem his brother as himself, and practice virtue and holiness before me. And again, I say unto you, let every man esteem his brother as himself" (D&C 38:23–25).

While helping is nearly always welcome, sometimes it can become condescending. We can think that we are better than others because they *need* our help and we have *bent down* to help them, perhaps even thinking, "Look what I have done for you."

Some years ago, a youth group visited a homeless shelter in Philadelphia that had a sign near the entrance that said this:

> If you are here to help us, we don't need your stinking charity. If you are here to learn about yourself; come, let's do it together.[3]

It's not the mere act of service that the Savior talked about but creating an attitude of helping that makes each of us a better person. In this way, the more we give, the more we learn about ourselves.

Activity: Creating an Awe Journal

Instructions

There are many different types of journals, including study journals, gratitude journals, and the more common daily journals. But "awe journals" are different from each of these other types.

Awe journals are best created with a camera phone and accompanying captions. The goal is to notice simple acts of helping and then take a photo so it can be remembered and shared. Even if it is somewhat after the fact, such photos can still capture the spontaneous feelings expressed by both giver and recipient. For children who do not have a camera phone, they can draw helping acts they observe in a notebook created just for "awe-inspiring moments."

3. Author experience as a Kellogg Foundation "Global Fellow."

Awe journals don't need to include daily observations or photos, but it is surprising how many "helping acts" occur all around us once we are attuned to noticing them. And by getting outside ourselves and watching what others do (unconsciously, modeling desired actions for us), we are better able to put into practice these same sensitivities.

In addition to the photos or drawings that family members create for an "awe journal," there are two other important components of this activity: writing captions and sharing observations with each other.

Writing captions gives expression to what we have seen and how we've felt. They make events more memorable for us. They become both personal and spiritual prompts. They allow us to look both outward and inward and say what something means to us. They don't have to be profound or wordy, just a few simple phrases will do. But these few words can be powerful reminders of what we observed and how we might emulate what we saw in others.

Debriefing

Sharing our observations with others lets us be "twice blessed." We can relive these experiences again and learn from each other what they may have noticed or some similar helping episode they may have captured. Sharing these observations increases each other's awareness and unselfishness without lecturing or micromanaging.

Here's some questions to consider when sharing observations with each other:

- What detail stands out about this photo or drawing?
- How are different people in the photo or drawing responding to what is happening?
- What do you imagine might have occurred just before you arrived on the scene? What was happening just before you took this photo or made this drawing?
- If you could change places with someone in the photo or drawing, who would you choose? What would you then do next?

Asking these types of questions promotes curiosity and can help family members turn a photo or drawing into an entirely new realm of possibilities.

Generalizing

Attitudes are formed from experience. Rather than simply talk about family members' attitudes, a more useful way is to create new experiences that allow them to form new or more helpful attitudes. We can develop new attitudes by observing other people, especially those we admire, and reflecting on how their actions might align with our own actions.

By discussing *helping traits* from "awe journals" family members are better able to support each other in creating *helping attitudes.* Such discussion after sharing photos/drawings and captions provides additional recognition and reinforcement. It's often easier to learn from each other in such indirect ways. Indirect learning occurs when family members observe, discuss, and draw inferences together. In such discussions, parents are facilitators who help highlight different points of view and possible implications rather than giving direct instructions or pressing personal points of view.

Applying

Sometimes we get bogged down in the day-to-day routine, doing the same things in the same old way. Tweens and teens can especially feel bored if not challenged with new experiences. Looking for "awe" and "wonder" in everyday events and activities not only gets them to think about others but also enables them to see for themselves the effect that it has.

Science is all about making observations and testing theories. It's the essence of curiosity. The more family members notice the world around them, the more likely they are to discover and learn about it. This applies equally to physical, social, and spiritual facts and conditions.

Rather than asking children, "How was your day?", parents can shift the conversation by periodically asking them, "Did you see anything 'awe-inspiring' today? Are you going to include it in your awe journal?" Since it is already an established topic, you can easily share observations and photos without waiting for a family council or family discussion.

SUMMARY

Sometimes "indirect learning" is the best way to help family members acquire a new skill, attitude, or mindset. Telling them to "be more helpful" is not as effective as allowing them to see for themselves the difference in the lives of others that helpfulness can make. Capturing real-time "awe inspiring moments" through a photo or a drawing is a kind of self-directed sermon delivered by family members to themselves.

Research has shown that children as young as three years of age feel better about themselves when they share.[4] And further studies show that participating in cooperative games and structured activities increase younger kids as well as teens' "prosocial behavior," such as being cooperative, kind, and sharing.[5] Further studies show that the more preschoolers feel secure in family relationships through such activities, the more they want to participate in them and these early learning experiences and the helpful attitude they develop persist with them even in later life.[6]

4. Cari Nierenberg, "Preschoolers Happier When They Share, Because They Want To," *Live Science,* 5 Jun. 2017, www.livescience.com.
5. M. Saleem, C.A. Anderson, and D.A. Gentile, "Effects of Prosocial, Neutral, and Violet Video Games on Children's Helpful and Hurtful Behaviors, *National Library of Medicine* (2012) 38:281–287.
6. "Benefits of Play," *Voice of Play,* www.voiceofplay.org/benefits-of-play, accessed Jan. 2023.

#18

Developing Mental Toughness

Mental toughness is used often in sports these days and more frequently in other family, school, and work settings. It is resisting or overcoming doubts, worries, or concerns while sticking to a task or schedule and persevering toward longer-term goals despite setbacks or naysayers. It is often used as a catchall term for such traits as resilience, grit, determination, fortitude, and tenacity when faced with overwhelming odds.

It is celebrated in successful athletes and scientists and increasingly with those with disabilities. It manifests itself in work ethic and daily habits, but it begins with self-identity: how we see ourselves. From a gospel perspective, it is a significant attribute in helping us return to our heavenly home.

In a Worldwide Devotional for Young Adults, President Russell M. Nelson emphasized that knowing three important truths make all the difference in starting and remaining on the right path:

1. Know the truth about who you are.
2. Know the truth about what Heavenly Father and His Son have offered you.
3. Know the truth related to your conversion.[1]

This focus on understanding both our personal identity and our longer-term possibilities is fundamental in developing the kind of mental toughness needed to stay on the covenant path. Overcoming self-doubts and listening

1. Russell M. Nelson, "Choices for Eternity," Worldwide Devotional for Young Adults, 15 May 2022, churchofjesuschrist.org.

to the promptings of the Holy Ghost rather than cynics or defeatists put us in charge of our eternal destiny.

INITIAL ASSESSMENT

There are a variety of pre-assessment questionnaires that can be used to determine the current mental toughness of family members. Here is a short listing of key assessment questions that in itself can be a useful family activity.

Yes or No

1. I'm very aware of how others are doing compared to me.
2. I'm often distracted by outside influences when taking a test, performing at a recital, or playing in a game.
3. I find it hard to try again when I have not done something well.
4. I dismiss well-intentioned people who encourage me as just uninformed well-wishers.
5. I set ambitious goals, then feel bad if I don't achieve them.
6. I don't like the pressure to perform in music, sports, school, or work.
7. The higher the stakes (recital, game, tests, etc.), the worse I perform.
8. I'd rather not set goals at all because then I don't have to deal with the fallout of not achieving them.
9. I don't like feedback or criticism even when it is well-intentioned.
10. I generally have more bad days than good days in a week.

While there's no "bright line" in determining mental toughness from this assessment, here's a general guide that can be useful in determining the status of each family member:

1–3 Yeses: Thriving
4–6 Yeses: Surviving
7–10 Yeses: Struggling

Activity: Try Something New

Almost any game or activity that is new to family members can be helpful in developing mental toughness. The goal is to encourage family members to get outside their comfort zone and simply try new activities. This Water Balloon Dodgeball game is one among many others that can be played together and then discussed afterwards to further mental toughness among family members.

For this game, get five water balloons per person along with two buckets/tubs with water so the balloons float and don't break prematurely.

Divide the backyard into two halves using a rope to mark the middle of the playing field. Put the two tubs/buckets in the middle of the playing field. Consider getting water balloons that are bigger, so they break easily on contact.

Water balloon dodgeball is just like regular dodgeball. Players race to get a water balloon out of one of buckets, then throw water balloons at each other from their side of the field (emphasize no head shots). When the balloons are gone, the team with the most players still in is the winning team.

Debriefing

Like any other game or activity, learning only occurs when later discussed and applied. When family members informally and collectively share observations and applications, they learn easily from each other. Since the focus of this activity is on mental toughness, the following questions can be used to highlight skills and habits associated with it:

- Were you aggressive or defensive in the game? How did that work out for you?
- What helps you take chances?
- Is that similar or different from what you typically do?
- Did you get upset at anyone on the opposite team?
- What emotions sometimes cause you to act out of character?

These are only some of the questions that may be considered and discussed. Depending on what happened and how family members reacted during the game, other questions may be useful. Importantly, as parents, try to avoid asking "leading questions" or making "should" statements." Instead, validate any feelings family members may express as well as help them consider other options when appropriate.

The primary purpose of debriefing is to "get everything out on the table." Anything and everything can be "grist for the mill" so to speak. But don't let negative feelings or emotions linger. Give them their due without dismissing them. Then, search for various ways to respond. This is where making generalizations comes in and may involve closer examination of various conclusions and alternatives.

Generalizations

The more family members dwell on distressing thoughts, the worse they will feel. This doesn't mean suppressing them. Quite the opposite, it means expressing them so they can be examined and, in many instances, shown for what they are: shadowy bogeymen that have no power or influence unless we give it to them. Rather than escaping discomfort or becoming anxious about trying new things, developing mental strength requires assessment and experimentation and often readjustment to find the right path forward. Here's some questions to help with that journey:

- What sometimes causes me to not try at all?
- What type of negative "self-talk" do I listen to most often?
- When that happens, what can I (what do others) do to redirect it?

Applying

Building mental toughness is taking control of your actions as well as your environment. Sometimes we may need to change what we are doing, while at other times we may just need to avoid places or situations that cause angst or diminish us. It's all about making conscious choices and not merely going with the flow. It's not always easy to determine which needs to change: your mindset or your surroundings. Sometimes, it takes a little experimentation. But in all cases, considering options and alternatives can be extremely helpful. Here's some questions that can help with that process:

- When do I seem to give up too soon?
- When do I hang onto a grudge or resentment long past its "expiration date"?
- When I feel inclined to hold back, what can help me try new things?
- What can I do when I start feeling sorry for myself?
- Who can help me experiment more with bouncing back when times are tough?

SUMMARY

Mental toughness is about persisting in the face of difficulties. Mentally tough kids will continue to do their best even when a goal seems difficult or so far in the future it's hard to see real progress in achieving it.

Recognizing obstacles in advance and encouraging persistence can be helpful. One way of doing this is to ask kids to write a letter to themselves about a goal they want to achieve and the type of obstacles they think they might encounter. Then they can say in their letter what they plan to do when that happens. Ask them to show their letter to another family member and get their advice on both the type of obstacles they might encounter and ways to address them when they occur. Whenever they feel like giving up on their goal, ask them to re-read their letter and update it with new ways to address old obstacles. This will generate motivation from within and enable them to push through difficulties they may encounter.

Mental toughness is about facing our fears rather than suppressing them. Recent surveys following the pandemic reveal that anxiety about the future among tweens and teens is higher than any point in the past century.[2] Youth stew about the future—a lot. Rather than dismissing these fears, parents can help family members confront them and then make decisions about what they would do in various defined situations: mistakes at school, poor health, job loss, environmental crisis, family illnesses, and the like. Asking "what if" and then brainstorming options together as a family not only promotes individual problem-solving but also reduces anxiety and stress.

2. Maria Abenes, "Teens in America: How the COVID-19 Pandemic is Shaping the Next Generation," *Psychiatric Times*, 12 Nov. 2021.

#19

Deciding You Can't Please Everyone

IT'S IMPOSSIBLE TO PLEASE EVERYONE ALL THE TIME. TRYING TO DO SO will only make you anxious and miserable. Yet, *people pleasers* abound. And the "membership fee" they pay for always wanting to be praised and accepted by others is exorbitantly high.

Yet, we grow up in a family where it's important to get along, to compromise, to put others' needs ahead of our own. So, how do we help our kids find the right balance between selfish and selfless and negotiate boundaries without kicking agreeableness into overdrive? For tweens and teens, acceptance and peer pressure can exert an even stronger influence than parents or teachers. What's to be done?

Telling family members to "calm down" and "don't worry about what others think" is probably the *least* effective approach. It's dismissive and demeaning. But simply passively listening and then acknowledging a family member's feelings is insufficient as well. Ultimately, helping family members *reframe* a pressure situation or even an ordinary one where it seems like they are being used as a "doormat," will lead to more success.

In the Seminary's *Doctrinal Mastery Core Document*, teachers are encouraged to show students how to "reframe the questions" they may have or situations in which they may find themselves by looking at them in a different way—with an eternal perspective.[1] Reframing happens when we adopt a different point of view.

1. "Acquiring Spiritual Knowledge," *Doctrinal Mastery Core Document* (The Church of Jesus Christ of Latter-day Saints, 2018), 4.

A popular example is a story told about a large truck that inadvertently was stuck in an overpass when its driver failed to notice the height restrictions. Several people, looking at the top of the truck stuck under the overpass, offered a variety of expensive and time-consuming ideas for remedying the situation. None were very satisfactory. Then, a small boy happened by and suggested taking the air out of the tires to lower the truck so that it could be easily moved from under the bridge. Being much smaller than the others, the boy had a different frame of reference and used this perspective to reframe the matter and offer a helpful solution.[2]

Sometimes reframing may also take *unlearning* something family members may have come to accept about themselves. This could include feeling a need to please others all of the time or feeling "secondhand guilt" when someone else does something wrong.

There are a few eternal principles that family members must fully embrace if they are going to recognize they can't be "all things to all people." Embracing these principles isn't a cure-all, but it is the first place to start. Some of these fundamental gospel principles are embedded in the following scriptures:

- "But behold he doth not command us that we shall subject ourselves to our enemies, but that we should put our trust in him, and he will deliver us." (Alma 61:13)
- "Trust in the Lord with all thine heart; and lean not unto thine own understanding." (Proverbs 3:5)
- "Let no man despise thy youth; but be thou an example of the believers, in word, in conversation, in charity, in spirit, in faith, in purity." (1 Timothy 4:12)
- "Watch ye, stand fast in the faith, quit you like men, be strong." (1 Corinthians 16:13)
- "Beloved, now are we the sons of God, and it doth not yet appear what we shall be: but we know that, when he shall appear, we shall be like him;" (1 John 3:2)

Reframing may require family members to give up some of their fears in order to become more self-directed. This can be hard. They don't want to hurt anyone else's feelings or get rejected by them or deal with conflict or differences or ever get criticized. It can seem awkward at first to speak up. And

2. "Can we just let the air out of the tires?" *PennState: Blog*, 26 Nov. 2013, https://sites.psu.edu/psych256all/2013/11/26/can-we-just-let-the-air-out-of-the-tires.

a little scary. After all, it's new and different and a little unpredictable. But just because it's awkward at first, doesn't mean it's not the best thing to do.

Changing a mindset, a habit, a way of seeing yourself and others, takes practice. Like learning to ride a bike, it may seem wobbly at first, but with practice it becomes second nature.

Activity: "Talk Back to People Pleasing" scenarios

Self-talk isn't just mindless chatter. It has a way of creating its own reality. In this activity, family members identify and then create various responses to *people pleasing* self-talk. They do this in five steps:

1. Identify situations when "people pleasing" is most pronounced.
2. Create absurd, over-the-top responses to what could happen by not going along with what others want.
3. Brainstorm options for other ways to respond.
4. Weigh options and select a tentative course of action with which to experiment.
5. Practice, through role playing, how using this response might play out.

Identify Situations

While identifying people pleasing situations can be done solely by family members, here's some possible scenarios to help get started that can either be adapted or get used as a catalyst. Use these to help create scenarios that work best for your family.

- I really need to study for a test but if I don't go to Celeste's house when she calls, she'll ask someone else and maybe she'll stop calling me.
- Shelly's pretty sarcastic and I don't like being around her but at least I'm not the butt of her jokes or pranks so I'm going to stay eating lunch with her because I don't want to be a target.
- I don't like the way the new kid is being treated but nobody listens to me anyway so I'm gonna just ignore the whole situation.
- I'm not going to join the math club because everyone will think I'm a nerd if I do.
- I don't want to be thought of as a "goody goody" so I go along with things that I don't think are right.

Create Absurd Responses

In order to avoid becoming ponderous or preachy in this activity, use humor to create ridiculous responses to each scenario. So, after identifying 3–4 situations to address with your family, then come up with as many outlandish and far-fetched responses or catastrophes as possible to reorient their thinking.

This is called "breaking set" in problem-solving and helps overhaul our mindset in creative ways. It's an exercise in helping family members see they may be going to extremes and can help them think differently about themselves and a situation. But it must be collaborative! Absurd responses are only helpful when done together.

Here's some examples of absurd responses using the scenarios just presented.

People Pleasing Situations	Absurd Catastrophes
"She'll stop calling me"	"That could be bad. Let's fantasize about a famous person she might call and their reaction!"
"I don't want to be a target"	"What's the biggest target you've ever seen? How far away could you stand and still hit it?"
"Nobody listens to me anyway"	"What if you had a dog whistle that only humans could hear? What would you use it for?"
"Everyone will think I'm a nerd"	"Interesting. If the school had a 'Nerd Day,' how would you celebrate it?"
"I don't want to be thought of as a goody goody."	"What would happen if you wore a sign to prevent that?"

Brainstorm Options

Brainstorming is thinking out loud without evaluation. It's getting lots of ideas on the table first, then evaluating them only after all possibilities have been included. Here's some questions to use as a brainstorming catalyst for these scenarios:

- What would happen if . . .
- How might a hockey player or fisherman or animal trainer think about this?

- If you had a million dollars to spend, how would you use it in this scenario?
- What's different about this from anything else you've ever known in your life?
- Who's a role model for this and how do they do it?

Weigh Options

There are many different ways to evaluate options. For this particular activity, use other family members who aren't directly involved in a particular scenario to weigh options and describe their reasons. In essence, they are acting as consultants.

This might be done by asking 3–4 family members to meet separately and discuss the pros and cons of each proposed course of action. In doing this, they can be most helpful if they consider the following:

- What's a positive step forward even if it doesn't completely resolve the matter?
- What's something easy to practice and do?
- What are some ways to get started speaking up, owning a situation, and deciding to take action?

Practice

Our inner voice can be powerful: either as a critic or a coach. In his book *Chatter,* University of Michigan psychologist Ethan Kross describes ways we can harness our inner voice to our advantage. Here's five key suggestions:

1. *Get a little distance*: Use your own name rather than "I" or "me" in your self-talk.
2. *Imagine advising a friend*: Separate yourself from the scenario so it is easier to consider new ways of dealing with an old situation.
3. *Zoom out:* Compare this situation to others you've successfully handled so that you leverage your own past experience.
4. *See it as a challenge*: Consider it something new and exciting to get better at rather than a threat.
5. *Travel forward in time*: Consider how things will look then if you've made some changes.[3]

3. Ethan Kross, *Chatter: The Voice in Our Head, Why It Matters, and How to Harness It* (Crown, 2021).

Families can use these suggestions when setting up role plays with each of these five scenarios (or others of your own creation).

SUMMARY

People pleasers have developed thinking patterns based on their fears which limit their ability to speak up for themselves and live true to their values. Tweens and teens are especially vulnerable to these patterns of thinking because they are influenced so much by their peers during adolescence. However, once they recognize that *pleasing people* is not an inherent personality trait but instead a way of thinking about certain situations, it is much easier to consider other options and reorient their self-talk.

Family members can help each other. They can provide a mirror to show each other what unrealistic fears or unlikely reactions they may be harboring. They can have "practice sessions" or dry runs with each other for different situations and evaluate them openly. They can channel self-talk productively instead of destructively.

It can be challenging to recognize that not everyone will like us. Sometimes, even doing the right thing may bring ridicule from others. Before David faced Goliath, he faced another bully in his own family who questioned his motives and accused him of neglecting his duties.

> And Eliab his eldest brother heard when he [David] spake unto the men; and Eliab's anger was kindled against David, and he said, Why camest thou down hither? and with whom hast thou left those few sheep in the wilderness? I know thy pride, and the naughtiness of thy heart; for thou art come down that thou mightest see the battle. (1 Samuel 17:28)

Resisting Eliab's accusations, David replied simply, "Is there not a cause?" (1 Samuel 17:29) and then, without arguing or second guessing his own commitment, went out to fight the giant Philistine.

#20

Cultivating Good Friends

In her book *The Science of Making Friends*, UCLA professor Elizabeth Laugeson notes that while some teens and young adults seem naturally to have *the gift of gab* in making friends, for most of us it doesn't come easily. However, by being aware of a few guidelines that can be taught and learned, children of all ages can get better at making and keeping good friends.[1]

There is an old adage that if you want a good friend, then be a good friend first. *For the Strength of Youth* describes it this way:

> To have good friends, be a good friend. Show genuine interest in others; smile and let them know you care about them. Treat everyone with kindness and respect, and refrain from judging and criticizing those around you.[2]

So, how can family members actually get started *being good friends* when they don't quite know where to begin? And beyond *telling* family members what to do, how can parents and teachers actually *help* younger and older children make and keep good friends?

Making and keeping good friends is both an art and a science. By combining the two together, family members can support each other in developing friendships.

It all starts by not trying too hard! There's really no substitute for being genuine and just being yourself. But whether or not we are aware of it, there are ways that we communicate being open and approachable or standoffish

1. Elizabeth Laugeson, *The Science of Making Friends: Helping Socially Challenged Teens and Young Adults* (Wiley, 2013).
2. *For the Strength of Youth* (The Church of Jesus Christ of Latter-day Saints, 2001), 16.

and uninterested. For instance, when others visit in the hall at school or church, do we join in or hold back? Do we jump into conversations only when they interest us, or do we participate regardless of the topic? Do we see ourselves as loners or insiders?

Body language communicates openness and accessibility more than any other factor, so help family members be aware of it and intentionally show they are approachable. Eye contact, open arms and palms, and a slightly forward leaning stance all show that a person wants to participate in a conversation or join a small group cluster.

Looking for *conversation starters* can also be helpful. For instance, noticing someone's jacket or shoes and saying something positive about them is a good way to get acquainted. Or wearing a t-shirt from another country or place can prompt others to ask about it.

These techniques can easily be demonstrated and practiced. They are simple and intuitive to some while they are less obvious to other children and teens. A good place to practice is with family members but extended family members can be particularly helpful as well. There is a built-in *social access factor* with cousins that can make it easier for family members to practice openness and approachability together.

Perhaps as much as anything else they can do, parents can make it easy to have friends over after school or on weekends. Making treats while not micromanaging the interaction are the hallmarks of parental involvement.

Activity: Trading Cards

The purpose of this activity is for each family member to describe what they would most like in a friend and what they have to offer a friend. Rather than make simple lists, however, family members create "trading cards" just like baseball or football trading cards with key factors on them for discussion and practice sessions. Here's how it works:

1. Give each family member a large index card-—ideally a 4x6 inch card.
2. Ask them to draw a "self-portrait" on one side with 1–2 distinctive facial characteristics, a nickname, and include 2–3 friendship characteristics from the "friendship well."

3. Put these words from a University of Minnesota survey about friendship traits[3] on Post-It notes for the friendship well. Then, tell family members they can only use 3 of them on the front of their trading card to describe themselves (add more of your own phrases or words, if desired).

- honest
- trustworthy
- loyal
- upbeat
- funny
- open
- compassionate
- original
- kind
- other-focused
- curious
- optimistic
- available
- reciprocal
- fair
- courteous
- reliable
- sensible
- accepting
- outgoing
- thoughtful
- spontaneous
- dependable
- decisive
- happy
- playful
- adventurous

1. Ask family members to select 1–2 of these traits they would like to be better at for creating friends and put them on the back of their card.
2. When complete, pass each trading card in a circular manner to another family member. On the back of the card, each family member either writes a suggestion about how to develop that trait or gives the name of someone in the neighborhood who is good at it that could be observed in the coming weeks for clues and helpful tips.
3. When the trading cards have made it around to each family member, it is returned to the "original owner." Each owner reads aloud all comments from the back of their card. The owner then picks one comment from the back of the card to explore further.
4. After picking a comment from the back of the trading card, the person who wrote that comment explains it further. In some cases, it may be helpful to have a "practice session" or role play demonstrating this trait. Any family member who feels comfortable demonstrating it in this practice session can participate.

3. Angela Novak Amado and Elizabeth Pell, "Friendship Matters! Improving Health and Well-Being by Supporting Relationships," *Impact* (29) 1.

Debriefing

After exploring ideas or traits together as a family, it is important to come back together to determine "What did we learn?" Without this kind of discussion and closure, an activity may be fun or interesting, but it is not a learning activity.

Learning activities require some synthesis of what happened and a resolve to apply learnings in a deliberate way. Here's a useful way to debrief this family activity together:

Sit in a circle with either a wooden log or a photo of a fire in the middle. Ask family members to imagine they are surrounding a campfire in the woods.

Ask each family member to talk about a time they made a new friend. Describe what happened in detail.

Then, ask the person on their right to add to their comment by answering some or all of these questions:

- What could help you do something similar?
- What might be difficult in doing something similar?
- Who could help you that seems a natural at making new friends?
- How will you determine when you are getting better at extending yourself to newcomers?
- What support would you like from other family members?

Generalizing

It can be difficult for teens to break out of familiar habits and make new friends. Parents and siblings can help, but sometimes the things we say are counterproductive. Telling an introverted teen to "just go start conversations" or "extend yourself to others" can seem more like nagging than supporting them in developing new friendships. Having role-playing exercises together involving typical situations as a family can be especially helpful.

Sometimes teens think that having lots of friends matter. But realistically, having a few reliable friends is much more important than lots of them. Its quality over quantity. Here's a few ways to develop new friends:

- Sit next to someone new at school.
- Wear a t-shirt with a catchy slogan and be prepared to say something positive about it.
- Help someone who needs directions while showing them the way rather than just telling them how to get there.
- Sign up for a school or class fundraiser.

- Listen to others comments in class and compliment them afterwards on their insights either verbally or in a text.

Applying

Make a wall chart with key observations and action items. Give each family member different colored stars. Ask them to put one of their stars next to an observation each time they put into practice something related to this comment.

Discuss creating and promoting friendship each month during a family dinner conversation or at some other time when the family is together.

SUMMARY

Friends do many things: boost our outlook, help us through rough spots, fulfill both physical and emotional needs. *For the Strength of Youth* emphasizes that:

> Everyone needs good and true friends. They will be a great strength and blessing to you. They will influence how you think and act, and even help determine the person you will become. They will help you be a better person and will make it easier for you to live the gospel of Jesus Christ.[4]

When kids go to school, they begin developing friendships that primarily involve doing things together. Parents can help facilitate this kind of "joining up" by hosting parties and activities at their home.

During adolescence, tweens and teens become more attuned to picking up social signals from peer connections that are stronger than any other time of life. "Friendship dramas" can be a big issue for tweens and teens. While parents may need to let family members resolve these dilemmas themselves, they can be a sounding board and problem-solving facilitators. By intentionally creating learning scenarios, family members can experience demanding situations in a safe family environment and discover new skills they can apply in everyday life.

4. *For the Strength of Youth* (The Church of Jesus Christ of Latter-day Saints, 2001), 16.

#21

Learning to Compromise and Adjust

There is a Ghanaian proverb that reminds us that "seeing for ourselves is better than being told by others." Learning to compromise and adjust is one of those skills that requires both seeing it in action and lots of practice to develop. Otherwise, it's just a trite tag line. Whether it's sharing a bathroom, playing a game because it interests others, or watching someone else's favorite movie, it is often easier to talk about compromising and adjusting than to do it.

Like teaching other life skills, the goal is not just to get kids to do something—not just *compliance*—but to change their mindset and help them *see* things differently. Without their agreement there is no commitment to change, only acquiescence.

Power struggles make compromise difficult. Emotions get heated. Tempers flare. Both sides dig in. Whether it's between parents and children or between siblings or others, difficulty comprising and adjusting typically boils down to "Who's in charge?"

We've all seen—and likely experienced—power struggles with other family members. These "battle of wills" often over trivial matters can seem silly to outsiders, but to the "contestants" who are directly involved, who wins and who loses matters enormously. It is all about face-saving and personal dignity. "I'm standing up for myself. I have my rights. You can't walk all over me." These are common, unexpressed sentiments. When any of us are forced to do something, we don't want to do, we rarely learn anything useful from it. Anger and resentment are the only real outcomes.

So, when a situation has emotions at a fever pitch, what's to be done? Say, "Calm down" or "You're just upset" or "Be the bigger person"? Do such labels and cliches ever really work? Unlikely. Yet, they are repeated often by parents or other family members trying to mediate a tension-filled situation.

While reducing emotions is important, how it's done makes a big difference. In her book *Kids, Parents, and Power Struggles,* Mary Kurckina differentiates between "emotion coaching" and "emotion dismissing."[1] Rather than *ignore* or *diminish* the power struggle, parents and others can instead *recognize* the situation may be about *self-respect* and then *coach* children in considering how compromising isn't about losing.

The ultimate goal of compromising isn't just to find a way out of a tense situation, but instead about simultaneously promoting self-respect while respecting others. Compromise isn't about "giving in" or "giving up;" it's really about "leveling up" to a better personal emotional outcome for everyone involved. In essence, both win-win emotional and situational outcomes.

Rick Warren, in his popular book *The Purpose Driven Life,* he says, "Humility is not thinking less of yourself; it is thinking of yourself less."[2] Rather than simply thinking "it's all about winning," it's instead thinking "how can we all win." Stephen Covey, who popularized the idea of an "abundance mindset" said that when we consider how we can "make the pie bigger for everyone" instead of "how do I get the biggest piece of pie myself" that suddenly changes everything, and we are able to see possibilities that were previously "hidden in plain sight."[3]

Once children, or any of us, see compromising as actually being more in control rather than less—of exercising the power to broker a deal rather than giving up—it not only becomes easier to adjust and compromise but also enhances our self-respect. Instead of "losing" we are actually creating the terms of agreement. What could be better than that!

While it helps to explain these concepts to family members, describing them isn't enough. They must be demonstrated and practiced. They must be seen to be believed. Family members must discover better ways than persisting in power struggles in order to adopt a more flexible approach to dealing with differences.

---

1. Mary Sheedy Kurcinka, *Kids, Parents, and Power Struggles: Winning for a Lifetime* (HarperCollins, 2000), 9–10.
2. Rick Warren, *The Purpose Driven Life: What on Earth Am I Here For?* (Zondervan, 2012), 149.
3. Stephen R. Covey, *The Seven Habits of Highly Effective People: Restoring the Character Ethic* (Simon and Schuster, 1989).

ACTIVITY: Compare/Contrast

Deep learning occurs best when accompanied by active learner problem-solving, a recent study reported in the National Academy of Sciences.[4] The more learners are asked to engage in a dialogue, make a choice, solve a problem, or report a personal observation, the more they learn.

In this activity, family members are asked to describe different ways they (or others) might respond to certain difficult situations. By identifying ways they could be seen as "giving up" or "giving in," they are then better able to identify alternatives that shape the outcome and promote self-respect. This compare/contrast activity helps family members see for themselves different ways of handling differences.

The following list asks family members to give examples of different types of responses to various scenarios.

	Types of Reactions	
	Give in/Give up	Shape Outcomes
You never seem to get to pick a family movie to watch.		
Your Mom is bugging you about homework again.		
Your sister keeps wearing your clothes without asking you.		
Your older brother is teasing you again because you are so short.		
Your sister is tattling because you won't give her the tv remote.		
Your brother left your shared bathroom a mess again.		
You hate watching cartoons, but you are babysitting and that's all your younger brother wants to do.		
Your friends want you to go to a movie with them, but your parents say it is too late.		

4. Wang, Minhong, et al., " Fostering Deep Learning in Problem-Solving Contexts with the Support of Technology," *Journal of Educational Technology & Society*, vol. 20, no. 4, 2017, pp. 162–65.

Debriefing

Siblings are going to disagree with each other, and parents and children are going to have conflicts. Figuring out how positively to deal with differences first, in your family, and, then elsewhere, is a critical life skill. In debriefing this activity, try to personalize. This can be done by writing each of these statements on an index card, then letting family members pick a card and respond to it.

What I argue the most about with my family is . . .

I feel like I need to stand up for myself when . . .

The time I got what I wanted was when . . .

I didn't like it when I had to . . .

The most difficult time for me to share is when . . .

Generalizing

Put these statements on Post-It notes and place them on a wall or poster board. Then, discuss as a family when each statement is consistent with gospel ideals and when it is not.

- If you don't stand up for yourself, no one else will.
- The meek shall inherit the earth.
- One for all and all for one.
- Winning isn't everything, it's the only thing.
- It's better to bend a little than break a relationship.
- It's always about his, hers, theirs, or mine.
- Kindness begins with me.

Applying

We all want to feel good about ourselves, to feel like our input matters, that we are respected for who we are. In power struggles, these sentiments get twisted into "winning at all costs." When parents see beyond the behavior family members might be exhibiting by acknowledging these underlying needs to be recognized and respected, then it is much easier to diffuse difficult situations.

This exercise helps family members understand and recognize the dynamics that may be involved in a power struggle. There are mixed messages that we often hear about "winning" and "losing" that can even make us reluctant to compromise or adjust to various situations. Unpacking what's really behind some of these societal messages can help us better align with gospel principles.

But it still may not be easy to avoid power struggles, a feeling about giving up or giving in, and shaping better options—especially when family members' blood pressure is already heightened in a given situation.

A simple reminder can be helpful. Try this one:

- *Unplug*: Take a step back, breathe deeply, look away for a moment.
- *Debug*: Ask yourself, What's really going on? What's really at stake here?
- *Restart*: Check signals together. What do we each want? How can we each get *some* of what we want?

SUMMARY

When locked in a power struggle, family members can find it easier to dig in their heels rather than compromise and reshape possible outcomes. Kids can especially have a short-term focus and only see conflict situations as a "life or death" struggle about who's going to be in charge, who gets to push each other's buttons, and who gets to drive the train—who gets to be "boss."

While differences are inevitable, animosity doesn't have to be. In Philippians we are encouraged:

> Let nothing be done through strife or vainglory; but in lowliness of mind let each esteem others better than themselves.
>
> Look not every man on his own things, but every man also on the things of others. (Philippians 2:3–4)

When we help family members consider what may be best for all involved, it changes their mindset. Tug-of-war type power struggles are replaced by a quest for the common good.

Many issues in families revolve around "Who's in charge?" Parents often feel that they must exert control and family members typically react to this by outwardly resisting or silently complying. The alternative is not permissiveness but equality, self-governance, and joint problem-solving. This is not a "technique" but instead a distinctive way of sharing responsibility in the family through intentional gospel living. It is continuously observing family interactions, discussing what works and why, and experimenting with the Word (Alma 32:27).

#22

Helping Kids Feel Safe in a Tumultuous World

Children can be deeply shaken and perhaps even silently distressed when they read about violence or disasters that are occurring in the world. They may wonder:

- What's coming next?
- Am I or my family at risk?
- Why do these bad things keep happening to innocent children and other people?

While doctrinally Church members may speak of calamities during the last days, to children these events from both the scriptures and the newspapers can seem overwhelming.

Words always matter. And while it may not be easy to find the right words, it is always worth the effort to discuss current events in an age-appropriate way with children by giving them some context for these events and helping them "unpack" difficult situations.

In general, the American Academy of Pediatrics recommends avoiding disaster topics with children under the age of 8. In most cases, they are too young to grasp the significance of them and the less said, the better. For older elementary school children, experts suggest limiting the information they share to a sentence or two, if possible. And, in particular, avoid showing photos or viewing details on television since these images can have a long-lasting adverse impact. For tweens and teens, they are likely to hear about horrific events among their peers so taking the time both to share values and listen to family members' concerns and impressions is important.[1]

Parents can use this type of rough age guide to determine how much detail to share with their children about a disastrous event. In addition to describing what happened in a particular disastrous event and how their children can protect themselves, it's also important to provide an eternal perspective about it. This can reduce fears, anxiousness, and uncertainty among family members.

Reading the scriptures together can help as well. We read in the Book of Mormon about a horrific event that occurred among the people Alma and Amulek were teaching who had believed their words:

> And it came to pass that they took Alma and Amulek and carried them forth to the place of martyrdom, that they might witness the destruction of those who were consumed by fire.
>
> And when Amulek saw the pains of the women and children who were consuming in the fire, he also was pained; and he said unto Alma: How can we witness this awful scene? Therefore let us stretch forth our hands, and exercise the power of God which is in us, and save them from the flames.
>
> But Alma said unto him: The Spirit constraineth me that I must not stretch forth mine hand; for behold the Lord receiveth them unto himself, in glory; (Alma 14:9–11)

While this scripture helps create an important context for difficult situations—our Heavenly Father receives innocent children and others to Himself in glory—merely talking about such crimes or disasters is not enough. In fact, commiserating over disasters or criminal acts may make things worse for children who are already on heightened emotional alert. Similar to other learning situations, family members learn best when they have the chance to experience and practice new skills in a supportive environment. Doing something together can be confidence boosting and fun if focused on "controlling the controllables" in family members' lives.

Just as schools and workplaces practice fire drills, so families can also simulate and practice safety drills. Beyond knowing what to do, such practice sessions also give family members confidence they can be "in charge" even when events or others' actions seem to suggest otherwise.

How these drills are discussed makes a big difference as well. Too much emphasis on "stranger danger" can make kids suspicious and wary of

1. Jeff Knutson, "Age-based tips and lessons to help students process upsetting events," Common Sense Education, 27 Jan. 2021, www.commonsense.org.

anyone and everyone, even those who might be helpful in a difficult situation. Rather than *disaster focused,* a better approach is to help family members be *helpers* and *heroes.* In other words, what can they do in any difficult situation to assess what's really going on and then improve things? Is that what helpers and heroes do?

This new focus changes family members from being mere objects or victims that are "acted up" to empowered advocates who "are permitted to act for [them]selves" (Helaman 14:30) in any situation. Rather than pushovers who ignore or go along with whatever others might be saying or doing, helpers and heroes find ways to make things better. Empowering children in this way turns potential scary situations into opportunities to make a difference.

Just like superheroes in the Marvel universe or everyday heroes in the newspaper, helpers and heroes not only are aware of what may be going on around them, but they also do something about alarming situations. They don't just stand by and watch. Instead, because they are prepared, they can take appropriate action.

Activity: Pushovers and Heroes

Lighten the mood for this serious topic by turning it into a game and thereby making it a little less intimidating. Do this by using index cards to write one of the following situations on each of them. Add others that are relevant and age-appropriate for your family. Make a game spinner with each family member's name on it.

The activity begins when family members draw a card and read it aloud. Then, they use the spinner to select one other family member to say, "Here's what a pushover would do in this situation" and then act it out between two family members. Afterwards, another family member responds with, "Here's what a helper or hero would do in this situation" and again it is acted out between two different family members.

Situations:

1. A man you don't know at a park says he's lost his puppy and asks for your help.
2. Your friend tells you how to go to suspicious websites without your parents finding out.
3. A classmate says he hates your teacher and angrily says she must pay for giving him a bad grade.

4. You get a text that says you've won $500 from a contest you didn't enter if you'll send $50 to them.
5. You are at the park playing with friends. Suddenly, lighting strikes one of them and they are unconscious.
6. Your friends are using facial recognition on some new website. They say privacy concerns are overstated.
7. You are home alone and see smoke billowing from the woods near your house.

Debriefing

This activity works best when family members both say what they would do and act out how they would respond. By comparing and contrasting "pushovers" to "helpers and heroes," family members can gain confidence and a skill set they may lack. Among the objectives of this activity is to help family members take a stand whether dealing with a disaster or an unusual situation of any kind. As the old saying goes: "prior planning prevents poor performance."

Here's some questions to consider when debriefing:

- What made you the most uncomfortable during any of these scenarios?
- What particular situations do you now feel more confident in handling?
- What particular situations would you like to discuss further?
- What other situations would it be helpful for our family to discuss and even act out?

Generalizing

The scriptures tell us that if we are prepared, we won't be fearful (D&C 38:30). Instead, we'll know what to do. We may not have all of the answers, but we can at least make a difference in a difficult situation.

Making a difference doesn't mean merely making a big splash. Usually, it's better to "look before you leap." Jerry Harvey, a family therapist, often says that it's useful to consider what "makes waves but leaves things unchanged and what helps drain the swamp."[2] Here's three ways to "drain the swamp":

- Stand back and ask: What are others saying or doing?
- Look around: How can I find out more?
- Look beyond the obvious: What could be helpful?

After considering these questions, family discussions could shift to include similar situations to those in the card game activity.

Applying

While we want to protect our children from harm or danger, hazardous situations abound. Helping family members develop simple rules to live by can assist them when faced with new or uncertain situations. Practicing with kids what they would do in realistic situations they may face can give them confidence they would not freeze up but would instead follow through using skills they have developed during role play sessions at home.

Sometimes it's difficult to have role play sessions at home with other family members who may embarrass or tease each other about their actions or responses. However, the more families engage in these activities, the easier it is for family members to stand up for themselves and develop their own "peer resistance skills."

Each time families practice what they might do in unusual or difficult situations, family members will become more confident in taking this same action when faced with similar dilemmas in real life. Talking about and then acting out what constitutes passive, evasive, or confident actions can help. Passive actions are simply going along with what others may say or do; evasive actions are ignoring or turning away from them; while confident actions are having a plan ahead of time and following through with it when faced with alarming situations.

Families can discuss frightful situations that may be age appropriate and then share examples of each type of reaction with specific examples.

Passive:

- What are examples of this?
- Do you ever feel that way?

2. Jerry B. Harvey, "Organizations as Phrog Farms," *Organizational Dynamics,* Spring 1977, kristinesargsyan.files.wordpress.com/2010/06/organizations_as_phrog_farms_by_jerry_harvey.pdf.

Evasive:

- What are examples of this?
- Do you ever feel that way?

Confident:

- What are some examples of this?
- What could you do when faced with this type of situation?
- Who else could help?

SUMMARY

Experts say that focusing too much on disasters, crimes, or scary situations can make children anxious and nervous if the focus is on "what can go wrong." Too much detail can heighten anxiety rather than relieve it. Find out what your children already know and let them ask questions. Be direct and to the point without "oversharing."

Without ignoring difficult situations, approach them in ways that build family members' confidence. This can be done in several ways:

- Practice family fire drills and then use them as a springboard to discuss other types of situations your children may be concerned about.
- Ask your children to draw a situation that they've heard about on the news that concerns them. Use this drawing to ask questions about it including what they might do if faced with a similar threatening situation.
- Put disasters in context. While they happen, and being prepared to address them is important, show how likely or unlikely similar situations are to occur with them.
- Remind them that they are never alone. Not only are other family members available for help and guidance, but the Holy Ghost will also help when called upon. We are never alone. He is our constant companion.

#23

Recognizing It's Not All about You

New York Times columnist David Brooks has written extensively on character development and today's societal trends. Recently, he cited a survey conducted among tweens and teens who overwhelmingly said they would rather be Justin Bieber's personal assistant than a research scientist or professor. It seems that celebrity status (or being near it) matters more than personal contribution, he notes.[1]

There is much said and written nowadays about *self-absorption* among today's youth. Their expectation for instant gratification and personal fulfillment is widely researched and well documented as a societal trend. But families can counter such influences with an intentional effort to develop perseverance, hard work, and personal drive.

Many researchers attribute the decline of these character traits to a shift of encouraging extracurricular activities and the decline of participation by children in doing household chores. A recent Braun Research poll found that fewer than 28% of parents today require their children to routinely perform household chores—even though 82% of these same parents said they were expected to do regular household chores growing up.[2] A 20-year study by Marty Rossmann at the University of Minnesota found the single best predictor of educational and career success among young adults in their

1. Paige Leskin, "american kids want to be famous on YouTube, and kids in China want to go to space: survey," *Insider*, 17 Jul. 2019, www.businessinsider.com.
2. Graciela Moreno, "Study says, chores = success," *ABC30*, 7 Nov. 2017, abc30.com.

30's was not family status, birth order, parenting style, or IQ but whether they grew up routinely doing household chores.[3]

Research reported by the American Academy of Child and Adolescent Psychiatry shows that children as young as age 3 can be given age-appropriate household chores that will develop important character traits fundamental to their overall development.[4] While some children are eager to help with household chores, others are not. Nevertheless, routinely requiring children to do household chores has been shown to:

- Develop organizational and time management skills
- Enable family bonding through shared responsibility for tasks
- Provide opportunities for success and parental approval
- Establish a foundation for independent living
- Enable conversations about expectations and completeness

Why is sweeping the floor, washing the dishes, and taking care of laundry so important to kids' well-being in life? One reason is that kids feel competent when they do their chores. Whether they're making their bed or vacuuming the floor, helping out around the house helps kids feel capable.

Doing chores also helps kids feel like they're part of the family, that others depend on them, and that what they do matters. These are life skills they are developing beyond the tasks they are assigned to perform. Giving children choices over time about when and what they do as well as rotating household job assignments among family members promotes both self-reliance and cooperative effort.

ACTIVITY: Who Would You Pick?

Put the names of each of the following 21 "paired sets" on a separate piece of paper and place them in a bowl or sack.

During this activity, each family member selects one "paired set" of names from the bowl or sack. Depending on the ages of the children, it may be helpful to provide a few words about each person's accomplishments in the "paired set," if needed.

3. Kimberly Dishongh, "Study finds having kids do chores is a good thing," *The Washington Times,* 12 Jul. 2015, www.washingtontimes.com.
4. "Teen Brain: Behavior, Problem Solving, and Decision Making," *American Academy of Child & Adolescent Psychiatry,* no. 95; Sept. 2017, www.aacap.org.

When a family member draws a "paired set," they pick which person they would like to spend a day with and give a short explanation including answering these three questions:

1. What characteristics do you admire about that person?
2. What questions would you like to ask them?
3. What would you most like to learn from them?

Paired Sets

- Abraham Lincoln or Thomas Edison
- Brad Pitt or Mahatma Gandhi
- Adele or Michael Jordan
- George Washington or Albert Einstein
- Alexander the Great or Winston Churchill
- William Shakespeare or Alexander Hamilton
- Leonardo da Vinci or Christopher Columbus
- Aristotle or Julius Caesar
- Amelia Earhardt or Martin Luther King Jr.
- Mother Teresa or Princess Diana
- Tom Brady or Harriet Tubman
- Nelson Mandela or Babe Ruth
- Thomas Jefferson or Issac Newton
- Wolfgang Mozart or Benjamin Franklin
- King Arthur or Helen Keller
- Joan of Arc or Johann Bach
- Oprah Winfrey or Neil Armstrong
- Eleanor Roosevelt or Warren Buffet
- Florence Nightingale or Steve Jobs
- Mary Todd Lincoln or Jacques Cousteau
- Madame Curie or J.K. Rowling

Debriefing

During this activity, family members can continue with additional rounds, if interested. Rather than getting into who family members *like* or *dislike, f*ocus on personal traits and attributes as much as possible. These may not be well-known but could form the basis of future research, follow-up, and discussion.

Once the family members have completed the rounds they have decided to participate in, take the time to look for any patterns.

- What type of people did family members pick most often?
- What traits were mentioned most often?
- What did family members say they would like to learn from the person they picked?

Write on a whiteboard or chart paper 2–3 key observations from patterns that family members noticed. Use these for later discussion.

Generalizing

Ask family members to pick one of the people they selected and go do some "fact finding" about them. Ask them to learn as much as possible about their childhood and early adult years.

- What was unusual or unique about their early years?
- What obstacles did they overcome?
- What personal characteristics of theirs do you want to emulate?

Applying

There is ample evidence to support the concept of role modeling, but less evidence on how it is actually done, how we are influenced by others, or how someone actually becomes a "role model."

Neuroscientist Matt Liebermann says that the process occurs when we are hardly aware that it is even happening. His research shows that the more we examine something or someone by gathering details about them or it—especially if we admire that person or thing—the more it sneaks into our brain and becomes a part of how we see the world.[5] Close examination increases the likelihood of someone becoming a role model.

Historical figures and others can become role models through close examination. The more family members are encouraged to find out about positive role models, the more likely they are to adopt similar traits or habits.

Families can use this activity to continue to learn more about the person they picked whom they most admired by having informal family discussions about them while driving in the car, visiting around the dinner table, relaxing together, or at the end of a day. Make it a fun activity by creating

5. Matt Liebermann, *Social: Why Our Brains Are Wired to Connect* (NY: Crown, 2013)..

collages with that person and posting them in family members' rooms or on a rotating family bulletin board.

Of course, this same research can be directed toward ancestors who may have lived at the same time who faced similar challenges or obstacles. The more personal traits and characteristics that are emphasized rather than achievements or accomplishments, the more likely historical figures or personal ancestors are likely to become meaningful role models.

SUMMARY

It's very difficult to read about someone else and grasp what's behind their drive and ambition. It's not the "what" they did but the "why" and "how" behind their actions that is key in helping family members develop these same traits. This can be turned into a simple plan by giving each family member an index card with the following key phrases:

What obstacles did this role model overcome?
Why did they pursue this course of action?
How did they do it?

The practical application of these what, why, and how principles is best applied in a practical way to activities family members are already involved with, including household chores, music practice, or personal projects. Delving into details about the role model's challenges and obstacles enables their life and personal traits to be included in family members' lives and applied in daily activities.

#24

Owning Up to Mistakes

"We all make mistakes" is a very common phrase. And it's true, we all make them. But saying that may not help us own up to the mistakes that we make. It's hard to take responsibility. More often than not, we want to excuse ourselves or blame others. We want to minimize our role or excuse ourselves entirely.

But not everyone is able to slough off a mistake easily. Sometimes, especially sensitive family members, we may believe we can never recover from a mistake. Both Alma the Younger and the Apostle Paul persecuted the Saints and did a ton of other bad stuff. But rather than dwelling on the past, they relied on their faith to help them focus on the future. And then they went out and did something for themselves and others.

There is a certain tyranny involved in "What if . . ." and "If only . . ." that can bind us to the past and prevent us from moving forward. We can "What if . . ." and "If only . . ." ourselves endlessly. Reminding ourselves that we are not things that happened to us, or even things we may have done, is one way to reorient ourselves and build on the past.

Susan Porter, General President of the Primary was asked in a 2022 Church New podcast how she, as a widow, could lead the Church's Primary organization. She replied that though she was someone who had experienced the passing of a spouse, that label didn't define her.

> I thought to myself, that's not who I am. That's an experience I've had, a very important experience, a very profound experience, but

> who I am is, I'm Susan, and I have certain strengths. I have certain weaknesses. That's who I am.[1]

She went on to say that we are not events that happen to us. Reminding ourselves that we are something more—eternally children of our Heavenly Father—enables us to reframe past situations, to externalize them rather than personalizing them, and look at them as we might examine a math problem or a story in a book. We can do this partially by referring to past mistakes as "it" or "them" to separate ourselves from these past events. Things didn't go the way we may have wanted them to go, mistakes were made, now what's next?

Dissatisfaction itself can be motivational when it leads to a desire to change and improve. But it can also lead to a "black hole" of self-doubt and self-incrimination. Listening to the words family members use is a clue to what they may be feeling and what course of action you might consider in helping them recover from a mistake. Here's a few common phrases and some indication of what may be going on with them:

Self-improvement	Self-doubt	Making excuses
"I messed up."	"I am a loser."	"It was unfair."
"It's not what I wanted."	"It'll never get better."	"It's not what they promised."
"I can see what I've done."	"I'm no good."	"They were wrong."

While parents will certainly want to respond empathetically in the moment to any of these statements, without dismissing them, such phrases also provide clues to the type of teaching moments they may want to create for their family. Rather than disagreeing with their children when hearing any of these statements ("Oh, that's not true"), not only can parents listen and ask further questions, but also use the information they gather for pointers and signals on what they should do next.

Some mistakes are the result of sin or disobedience to the commandments. But not all mistakes are sins and should not be confused with wrongdoing. Sometimes we just mess up and are embarrassed by something we did, or maybe something we didn't do. At other times, we just may forget.

1. Sarah Jane Weaver, "Episode 93: New Primary General President Susan H. Porter on how teaching and serving children can be life-changing," *Church News: Podcast,* 19 Jul. 2022, https://www.thechurchnews.com/2022/7/19/23278315.

Or we didn't notice something. Or we dropped the ball at a crucial point when others were watching.

It all depends on the mistake, of course. Genuine repentance is required for sin—which means we must "confess and forsake" (D&C 58:43) before moving on. But for other mistakes and embarrassing acts, we may simply need to find ways to acknowledge what we've done and then look for ways to resolve them with friends, family, or others.

An effective way for parents to teach their children how to take responsibility for mistakes is to use conversation cards that have real-life scenarios for family discussion.

Many businesses and other organizations conduct "scenario planning" to rehearse what they might do in various types of emergencies. The Church creates scenario plans that local members may participate in to handle such things as fires or floods in a local area or public threats or other difficult or unusual situations. Such scenario planning helps us consider options ahead of time so that when the pressure of an actual challenging situation occurs, we can call upon past discussions or experiences to inform our current actions. We can be more intentional and less reactive, more thoughtful without flying by the seat of your pants.

There are many different types of conversation cards that are professionally produced and can be purchased online or in-stores. However, parents can also develop their own set of conversation cards with applicable scenarios based on their family's needs and any information they've gathered about their children's tendencies toward self-improvement, self-doubt, or making excuses.

The following scenarios are a "starter set" of conversation cards that you can add to with additional scenarios that you create. You can print each scenario on card stock and use it by shuffling all of the cards and letting each family member pick one at a time from the deck. There's something about the randomness of picking a card and reading it aloud that not only makes the discussion easier, but also more fun and less staged—especially for teenagers.

Activity: What's Wrong

So, here's an initial set of scenarios and some discussion questions (and tips for using them) that you might consider using along with the scenarios.

SCENARIO #1

You rode the bus to school today and on the way other kids began pointing and snickering at you. At school, you go to the bathroom and find that you have gum on the back of your pants.

What's your initial reaction?

Allow your children to comment without agreeing or disagreeing with their comments. At this stage, encourage them to open up and say what they think their initial reaction would be without passing judgment on their remarks. Let them express embarrassment or frustration or dismay without being dismissive of their feelings.

What would make things worse if you did them?

Sometimes, letting children explore the *worst* things they could do makes it easier for them to discuss later more productive responses. If possible, add funny or unusual or outlandish ways to respond to stretch their imagination.

What are better ways of responding?

Depending on the discussion, you may need to "prime the pump" by sharing your own experience or the experiences of other extended family members with a similar situation. We all like a good story. Even better if we can identify with those who are involved. But try to keep it "real" and avoid simply relating dissimilar situations with predictable answers.

SCENARIO #2

You wake up and see that your alarm never went off. You have a really important test during the first period of school and you cannot be late. Your teacher is very strict. But, at this point, there is no way that you can make it to school on time. What could you do?

Is it better to go to school late and take your chances or call in sick?

Life is full of dilemmas like this. How many times we choose a particular course of action ultimately determines our character. Virtue isn't always rewarded on the spot. But virtue is its own reward.

Would immediately calling your teacher or sending a text make a difference?

No one really likes being late. How often you've been late in the past will likely have a big impact on how things go this time around.

Scenario #3

You are giving a group presentation in front of class and it's your turn to talk. All of a sudden, you sneeze. You cover your nose and mouth with your hand, but now your hand is full of stuff you sneezed out. What could you do?

Do you acknowledge something is amiss or just ignore it?

With any awkward situation, the big question is whether to acknowledge it or pretend nothing happened.

How will you know when it's been forgotten by others?

Rather than telling kids "It'll all be forgotten soon," instead allow them to proactively determine when they think it will be water under the bridge. How will they know? This also shifts gears from self-recrimination to problem-solving. It gives them an active role in seeing for themselves that most embarrassing moments pass quickly.

How did you handle other types of embarrassing situations?

This is an especially good family or group question so that others can share their own experiences and share real life experiences together.

Scenario #4

You are eating dinner at a fancy restaurant with your parents and their friends. You have a really messy dinner and accidentally flip a noodle onto the backside skirt of your mom's friend. They are busy talking and she doesn't notice it. What could you do?

We all want to make a good impression, so how might this situation be turned from a negative to a positive?

In a world where everyone feels pressure to be perfect, there's real value in admitting that you're only human. When you can laugh at your own mistakes and get other people to laugh at them too, that helps give you the confidence to move past them.

What makes it easier to laugh at yourself when making a mistake?

There's an old saying that "laughter is the best medicine," but it's not always easy to laugh at ourselves. Saying "whoops!" or "Would you look at that?" or "Oh, my goodness, I've done it again" are disarming ways to initiate self-deprecating humor. Sometimes, using little starter phrases like these can help. Asking "*What are some other things we might say when inadvertently we mess up in front of others?*" can help family members see how others handle such situations and help them to use their experience when awkward situations occur.

SCENARIO #5

You are hanging out with your friends walking home along the sidewalk in your neighborhood. Your best friend decides to pick your neighbor's flowers. She gives you a handful of flowers just as your neighbor opens the door. Your neighbor is upset and asks you why you picked her flowers? Your friend is looking down at her shoes but not saying anything.

What would you say to your neighbor?

Even if you did not pick the flowers, if you were there when it happened, you might be considered an extension of another's actions.

Would you tell your neighbor you didn't do it and risk getting your friend in trouble or would you take the blame and try to talk your way out of it?

What might you do or say to your neighbor to make amends?

While initially upset, your neighbor might appreciate things that you could do later such as planting flowers to replace those you picked or writing a note to apologize.

What might you do next time?

It's hard to learn from our mistakes, especially when we are concerned about what others might say or think. Teenagers are particularly susceptible to the opinion of their peers. If you have a story or experience where you said you weren't going along with what a friend started doing and how that helped both of you, share it with your children.

SUMMARY

When mistakes cause us to feel like we are failures, we are less likely to own up to them or to learn from them. Perfectionism gets in the way of learning from experience. Telling family members not to be so hard on themselves, however, is unlikely to be very effective in addressing perfectionism, either.

Here's a few tell-tale signs of perfectionism especially among tweens and teens:

- Needing to ask a lot of questions "to get it right" when given a task.
- Being inflexible or believing there's only one right way to do a task.
- Becoming very self-critical when not meeting their own high expectations.
- Procrastinating to avoid difficult tasks for fear they might fail.

So, if perfectionism is often the root of an unwillingness to own up to mistakes, what can parents do? Here's some suggestions:

Praise effort, not results.

If parents are hyper-focused on achievement, then children will become very averse to mistakes. They will be more likely to do things they can accomplish easily, rather than risk falling short. Try saying things to your children like, "You really tried hard at that. How does it make you feel knowing that you've persevered despite obstacles?" This allows the child's own internal motivation to kick in rather than praise only coming from you or others.

Discuss famous failures.

Abraham Lincoln lost seven elections before he was elected President of the United States. Edison had multiple failures before perfecting the light bulb. History is full of examples of people who failed multiple times before they finally gained success.

Ask: What would you say to a friend?

A good way to externalize perfectionism is to ask a child to say what they would tell a friend who felt as they did. Considering their response to others can then help them apply this advice to themselves.

Avoid toxic positivity.

Attempting to minimize perfectionism is likely to backfire. While it's not healthy to wallow in shortcomings, it is vitally important to acknowledge and validate them to give sufficient personal space for self-examination. It's all about balance. As Elder Neal A. Maxwell once said, even gospel standards are "stars to steer by, not stripes to beat ourselves."[2]

2. Barbara B. Smith, "A Conversation with Sister Barbara B. Smith, Relief Society General President," *Ensign*, Mar. 1976, 7.

#25

Fostering Positive Relations with the Opposite Sex

As tweens and teens grow, they naturally want to explore relationships with members of the opposite sex. At any age, healthy relationships with others promote balance and enhance personal development. Unhealthy relationships are all about exclusivity and lopsidedness, whether among tweens and teens or even longer married couples.

Finding just the right balance can be tricky at any age. But among teens in particular, hormones and a sense of awkwardness can play havoc with finding such harmony. There is a tendency for peers to create implicit pressure to do certain things by a certain age. Social media can intensify this subliminal pressure, making it more difficult for them to "find their own way."

Of course, navigating this new stage in life can be just as challenging for parents as it is for tweens and teens. How families relate and deal with this "new factor" affects so many other family dynamics that it's hard not to overestimate its importance. And while parents may feel like their past experience is enough to help them advise their children, the social landscape for tweens and teens has changed dramatically in recent years and we are often woefully out of date.

According to surveys conducted by the Department of Health and Human Services, the number of kids who graduate from high school without ever going on a date has more than doubled in recent years: from 14%

to 38%.[1] Kids are more prone to "hang out" in their bedrooms or elsewhere rather than even go on a group date nowadays. Of course, mobile phones and social media make visiting with others both easier and less personal. Researcher Dr. Delaney Ruston notes in her book *Parenting in the Screen Age* that even when together, teens and tweens may spend more time scrolling or using electronics than interacting with each other.[2] More than ever, times are changing. And keeping up with this new environment can be both breathtaking and scary for everyone.

While getting over-involved—or just being plain nosy—with a tween or teens "romantic interests" can be counterproductive, so can remaining passive or standoffish. Kids want to talk to their parents about what's going on in their lives—including their relationship attractions—but they want to do it on their own terms. How parents *listen* as well as *advise*—start conversations or ignore delicate topics, engage or remain aloof, pry or neglect—are all factors that determine what kids will share with their parents and what they keep to themselves.

During the tween and teen years, it's more important than ever to be intentional in talking about how to develop positive relationships with members of the opposite sex. If parents don't find a way to discuss such relevant topics, someone else will!

If the landscape has changed with social media and mobile phones, so too has the language. Nowadays, it's all about who has a *crush* on whom and whether or not someone is "into you." And it is even what a *crush relationship* means including whether or not it is reciprocated. Having a crush can have a wide range of meanings and expectations from infatuation to flirtation to getting serious that only those directly involved grasp. But, at least, getting the lingo down is a good first start for parents.

Almost everybody has multiple crushes in their teenage years. In fact, having lots of them is better than having one or none at all. Just as there are many different types of crushes, so there are lots of ways of dealing with the feelings that accompany them:

- Ignore them
- Fantasize and daydream about them
- Stay guarded and keep your distance
- Stick to friendship

1. "Healthy Relationships in Adolescence," Office of Population Affairs, opa.hhs.gov/adolescent-health/healthy-relationships-adolescence, accessed Jan. 2023.
2. Delaney Ruston, *Parenting in the Screen Age: A Guide for Calm Conversations* (Starhouse Media, 2020).

- Tell the person about them

There's no "one right way" for dealing with crushes. In fact, any of these approaches may be the best one for any particular crush. But helping teens reach outside their comfort zone and figuring out what may be possible is worth the effort. You may surprise even yourself.

HOW TO READ THE SIGNS

Helping youth learn to read the signs in a developing relationship with a member of the opposite sex is an easy way for parents to talk with them about "crushes" and turn a potentially awkward topic into an open dialogue.

Here's some questions parents might discuss with family members in developing positive relationships with the opposite sex:

- Do they hang back to visit with you after class?
- Do they respond to texts?
- Do they follow you on Facebook or Instagram?
- Is there much eye contact when you are together?
- Can you tell if they are nervous and shy or just uninterested?
- Are you comfortable or uneasy with each other?
- Are they mostly on their phone when you are together?
- What's their motive: friendship or something else?
- What does their body language suggest: bored or interested?
- Do you feel nervous, queasy, or excited when together?

HOW TO CREATE SPARKS

Every relationship has its highs and lows and learning to navigate them for teens takes time and practice. While boys are typically awkward in social relationships with girls in their early teens, all youth can learn to relate easier to others with a little practice and support. Here's some questions parents might discuss with their teens to help them become more comfortable in a new relationship.

- What kind of compliments would they most appreciate?
- What interesting stories can you share online or in person that interests both of you?
- How can you connect personally when at church or school activities?
- What do you have in common that you can do together?
- What conversation starters and open-ended questions can you use to help with "awkward pauses"?

Research from York University, reported in the Church News, has confirmed the benefits of a natural progression of informal activities between girls and boys as they enter Young Women and Young Men activities leading to regular, structured group activities after they turn 16 and begin to date.

"It's important for parents to monitor the type of relations [their] teens are involved in and to promote activities that bring boys and girls together in fairly structured, supervised ways," said Jennifer Connolly, a professor of psychology at York University. Her research shows that those who form romantic one-on-one dating relationships young are more likely to have problematic behaviors at school and in other areas of their lives. She suggests that parents might consider how they can facilitate such interactions for awkward teens.[3]

Activity: Cooperative Board Games

Adolescence is a time for learning and discovery. The more tweens and teens broaden their relationships with others their same age, the better prepared they are to interact with others as adults. The Church's *For the Strength of Youth* notes that: "Developing serious relationships too early in life can limit the number of other people you meet and can perhaps lead to immorality."[4] Rather than becoming narrow and exclusive, the more youth broaden and include others in their circle of friends, the easier it is to relate to others from different backgrounds later in life.

Playing cooperative board games is among the best ways to broaden and deepen relationships without putting them under a microscope. Seeing how others react in different game situations—and whether they are respectful of you and your perspective—is one of the best ways to determine if this is a relationship worth investing more in or if it's better to limit it.

Here's some great board games to play as well as use as "lightning rods" to see if there are any "relationship red flags:"

- *Pandemic* A cooperative game of teamwork for two to four players or teams. As members of an elite disease control team, you must keep four deadly diseases at bay. Work together as you travel the globe to treat infections while collecting the cards you need to

3. Lois M. Collins and Marianne Holman Prescott, *Dating, courtship*, Church News, https://www.thechurchnews.com/2014/1/4/23223682/dating-courtship, accessed Oct 4th 2023.
4. *For the Strength of Youth* (The Church of Jesus Christ of Latter-day Saints, 2011), 4.

discover a cure for each disease. But the clock is ticking as outbreaks and epidemics fuel the spreading plagues. As a cooperative game, players win or lose together. Only by working together can you keep the outbreaks in check and find the cures in time!

- *Unlock: Timeless Adventure* This game captures the excitement of a physical escape room adventure without leaving the tabletop. With one hour on the clock, players work through a deck of 60 cards to solve puzzles. Once the team enters the correct code into the companion app, they win!
- *No Thanks!* This game has simple rules and moves very quickly. It isn't a "thinking" game but has some strategy elements. It is a game of "pushing your luck" when making choices about each card that a player draws. During play, each player chooses either to accept or pass (say "No Thanks") to a card that is face down. Passing increases the number of "chips" associated with that card. Lowest number of chips at the end of the game wins. Its all about making decisions with limited information.
- *Escape—The Curse of the Temple* In this game, players simultaneously roll their dice and look for particular symbols to unlock doors and move into rooms. However, players will have to be careful not to remain out of the central chamber too long. Throughout the game, a musical track will play— which does a lot to help with the immersion—which will signal to players when they need to start making their way back to the central chamber.
- *Robinson Crusoe: Adventures of the Cursed Island* There are six phases in each round of the game: Event, Morale, Production, Action, Weather, and Night. Three different sets of dice are used for each of the three actions in the game (building, gathering, and exploring). The dice will tell you if an action is successful or not (success, wound, or adventure).

Debriefing

Discussing ways to develop positive relationships with the opposite sex with teens can be challenging. They want their independence and don't want their parents to be nosy or give too much advice. Because the world is changing rapidly, they may not feel like you understand their pressures and circumstances. And likely, you don't! —which can be to your advantage as a parent. It can make it easier for you to be a *sounding board* and explore this unfamiliar territory together.

As a sounding board, parents don't need to have all of the answers. In fact, you don't need any answers at all! But having some helpful questions can be useful. After playing a board game and when others have gone home, here's some ways to talk about the time they spent together:

- Who seemed the most respectful of others' ideas and input? What did they do?
- Did anyone get upset or angry? What red flags might this raise?
- Did you notice anyone dismissing the ideas of others?
- Did someone play like they had to win? What did they do?
- Was there any "drama" while playing the game?
- Who encouraged others the most? Who just sat back and watched?

Generalizing

It's easy to overlook "clues" about others' tendencies and reactions to events. Debriefing helps but we can all misinterpret others' intentions or motives. First impressions are often wrong. Taking the time later to check out initial impressions ensures that we don't draw inaccurate conclusions. In generalizing, the goal is to look for patterns and withhold judgment until there's enough information to draw a valid conclusion.

Relationship coaches often challenge the conclusions that others reach. Parents can do the same thing. But timing matters. Most of the time, family members won't be open to new ways of seeing things until they've had a chance to fully explain how they see things. But empathy alone isn't enough either. It's a first, essential step, but must lead somewhere. Helping family members check out impressions is an especially useful way parents can be sounding boards.

- What did you see in others who played the game you hadn't noticed before? What do you think that means?
- How can you further check out these impressions?
- Who's a trusted friend that you can ask if that seems right or not?
- What are some of your natural tendencies or filters that might be a factor?
- What's the best way that I can help you with this right now?

Applying

Like other skills, there's a natural progression in developing positive relationships with members of the opposite sex just like learning to crawl, then walk, and finally to run. Discovering how to better interact with others takes reaching out as well as figuring out how best to connect with members of the opposite sex. Using others as a sounding board helps all along the way. Here's some questions to get started that can be used as prompts in such a dialogue:

- What would make you more emotionally confident with members of the opposite sex?
- What could help you talk more easily to other members of the opposite sex about your values and the positives in your life?
- Who can you depend on to keep a secret?
- Who/What are your best "lifelines"? Do you use them with simple relationship matters when needed?
- How can you use the scriptures and relevant topics in *For the Strength of Youth* for guidance?

SUMMARY

In so many ways, parents intentionally or unintentionally model in their own relationship with each other what their children perceive as positive or negative, healthy or unhealthy. One of the single best ways parents can help teach healthy relationships with the opposite sex is to show affection to each other. Touching, hugging, and gentle caresses with each other are noticed and set a tone in the home.

Kids, too—at any age—crave and respond to affection. At times, they may resist it or say that they are too old for such things. But research shows that tweens and teens actually want an arm around the shoulder more often than they get it. According to family therapist Virginia Satir, just like daily vitamins, everyone (including teenagers) needs four hugs or affectionate touches a day from someone just for survival in our less-than-personal world. Beyond survival, eight hugs or touches are needed for personal maintenance and twelve daily hugs or affectionate touches are needed for the kind of emotional security that facilitates personal growth.[5] No wonder Jesus healed the sick most often by touching them. Then, when He appeared in the Americas, He asked the assembled congregation to come forth and

5. Virginia Satir, *The New People-Making* (Chicago: Science and Behavior Books, 1988).

touch Him by feeling the prints of the nails in His hands, feet, and side. He touched others. They touched Him.

While tweens and teens want affection from parents and others, they want it on their own terms. Most of all, they don't want to feel like they are being treated like a small child. Worse. Asking what they like won't help, either. They probably don't know. So, try various things—tussling hair, giving finger taps on their shoulder, grabbing a hand when going out the door—and see what is welcomed and maybe even gets reciprocated.

Feelings toward "crushes" may not be reciprocated either but having such relationships—even when limited—are still important in adolescent development. Rather than discouraging them, parents should guide family members in dealing with them—the highs and the lows. This doesn't mean "popping their bubble" by saying they may not last, but instead listening and supporting and not getting involved in talking about them. Without various infatuations or fleeting "crushes" —some which may turn into long-term relationships or even marriage—teens miss an important developmental milestone.

Being available to talk and to listen, to validate and to explore, to encourage and to remind them *who they are* is what growing together as a family and being there for each other is all about.

#26

Discovering What You Are Good At

"WHAT DO YOU WANT TO BE WHEN YOU GROW UP?" IS A COMMON QUESTION to kids of all ages. Sometimes, adults too ask themselves the same question. It's not altogether a bad question, but, to some extent, it's not a very good one, either.

Why? Because it forces kids to choose an answer when they don't know that much about their options. It implicitly says they *should* know what they want to be even at a young age and so they pick something familiar just because it's handy. Then, without realizing it, they only pursue that option without looking into others.

Even worse, it creates idealized versions of real life. What kid ever says they want to be a welder or a UPS delivery truck driver or postal worker? Instead, kids pick high status jobs—doctor, lawyer, astronaut—when they may have little interest in doing the day-to-day tasks that go along with that type of job.

While study after study among parents say they just "want their kids to be caring and happy," when these same researchers ask the kids what their parents are telling them, the kids say their parents focus mostly on success and achievement. It's not a mixed message, it's a single-focused one.

When Elder Dallin H. Oaks was President of BYU, he encouraged students to broaden their possibilities and not pick a career until they had thoroughly considered multiple options. As an example, he said he was a second semester sophomore before deciding to pursue a career as a lawyer.[1]

1. Personal interview with the author.

We all have unique talents and abilities. Some of them are obvious, others may be hidden. Some may be well-compensated in the world of work; others may provide lots of personal satisfaction but less remuneration. Importantly, doing what we *like* to do not only helps us find *joy in the journey* but likely leads to better compensated work simply because we tend to do well at things that we enjoy doing.

Besides, who knows how work will change in the future and what kind of occupations will emerge that no one even knows about today? If someone asked Steve Jobs or Phil Knight or Elon Musk or many others "What do you want to be when you grow up?" would their answers have anything to do with their career path? Likely not.

Asking family members too often "what do you want to *be*"—an endpoint—can even obscure a much better question, "What do you like to *do*?"—those activities that challenge, invigorate, and expand those often innate but hidden abilities.

Here again, family members may have limited experiences and hardly be aware either of what they like to do or what they may be good at. So, rather than jumping quickly to a few comfortable activities as a reference point, perhaps looking for ways to try out new and different skills and more thoroughly assess aptitudes may be required.

It can be challenging to help family members find their innate abilities that are also marketable. This matching process is complicated by unclear work and career options as well as unidentified personal skills and interests.

So, what's to be done?

Activity: Holland Self-Directed Search

Perhaps more than anyone else, Dr. John Holland and his colleagues at Johns Hopkins University have studied the relationship between our personalities and interests and possible career options. More than 35 million people have taken the Self-Directed Search career assessment and exploration tool they created.[2] Portions of it are even used in the Church's self-reliance materials and included in youth-oriented Church magazines.

There are shorter as well as more involved versions of the Self Directed Search assessment. Here is an abbreviated version that families can use in getting started. More detailed version is available at www.self-directed-search.com

2. See https://self-directed-search.com/

Instructions

Read each statement. If it is something that you like to do regardless of your proficiency, background, or training, circle the number beside the statement. If it's not very appealing to you, just pass on it. There's no wrong answers and no advantage either in circling a lot or just a few statements.

I like to work on cars.
I like to do puzzles.
I like to work independently.
I like to work in groups.
I am an ambitious person with many high goals.
I like to organize things (files, desks, offices).
I like to build things.
I like to read about art and music.
I like to have clear instructions.
I like to try to influence or persuade people.
I like to do experiments.
I like to teach or train people.
I like to help others solve their problems.
I like to take care of animals
I wouldn't mind working 8 hours a day in an office.
I like selling things
I enjoy creative writing.
I enjoy science.
I am quick to take on new responsibilities.
I am interested in healing people.
I enjoy trying to figure out how things work.
I like putting things together or assembling things.
I am a creative person.
I pay attention to details.
I like to do filing and typing.
I like to analyze things (problems/situations)
I like to play instruments or sing.
I enjoy learning about other cultures.
I would like to start my own business.
I like to cook.
I like acting in plays.
I am a practical person.
I like working with numbers or charts.
I like to get into discussions about issues.
I am good about keeping records of my work.
I like to lead.
I like working outdoors.
I would like to work in an office.
I'm good at math.

I like helping people.
I like to draw.
I like to give speeches.

Now, tally your response: Mark if you circled "yes" to the numbers in each category in the columns below, then tally how many yeses in each category:

Realistic:	1, 7, 14, 22, 30, 32, 37
Investigative:	2, 11,18, 21,26, 33, 39
Artistic:	3, 8, 17, 23, 27, 31, 41
Social:	4, 12, 13, 20, 28, 39, 40
Enterprising:	5, 10, 16, 19, 29, 36, 42
Conventional:	6, 9, 15, 24, 25, 35, 38

These six basic "orientations" describe primary *interests*, they are not about *skill levels* or *abilities*. Since we tend to do better at tasks that we enjoy, the more we can find jobs or occupations that interest us, the more likely we are to enjoy what we do and then do it well.

Holland suggests focusing on a primary and secondary interest category. So, the category that received the most "yeses" is your primary interest and whatever received the second most "yeses" is a secondary interest to consider. Here's the types of jobs or careers that match up best with each of the six "interest orientations."

REALISTIC—This interest orientation involves the use of tools, machines, or other physical skills. Careers working with plants and animals, being out-of-doors, and building things appeal to those who score high in this area.

INVESTIGATIVE—These types of jobs involve theories, research, and intellectual inquiry often with a focus on science, technology, and medicine.

ARTISTIC—A high interest in art, design, language, and self-expression while typically working in an unstructured environment producing something unique.

SOCIAL—Typical jobs involve teaching, coaching, and advising other people while working in a cooperative environment.

ENTERPRISING—These jobs involve leading, motivating, and influencing others while working with others to get things done.

CONVENTIONAL—These jobs involve managing data, information, and processes.

This is a broad assessment that can be helpful in determining what type of career might be most appealing and, consequently, is a good place to start when trying to discover what you are good at. The Holland Self-Directed Search provides a brief introduction to discovering personal interests and starting to match them with career options. Taking the full-scale version can further your assessment and exploration. The website www.self-directed-search.com provides a fuller version of this introductory assessment and gives many other related suggestions.

ACTIVITY: Informational Interviews

While the Self-Directed Search assessment can be very helpful, it still gives only general direction rather than specific suggestions. A way to narrow potential career options even further is by conducting *informational interviews.*

These are semi-structured conversations with someone in an occupation that matches a family member's interests from the Self-Directed Search. While almost everyone will talk about the reasons they went into a particular field, practicing a little probing with other family members will make these interviews much more productive. Here's how to make the most of them.

1. Identify several types of jobs/occupations that may be of interest.
2. Do some homework to find out educational or other basic requirements and ask about them.
3. Identify 2–3 different people who are working in the field.
4. Develop a list of questions to ask each person so that you can compare responses later. Here's a starter set:
    a. *How do you get into this line of work?*
    b. *What do you enjoy about it?*
    c. *What's not so great about it?*
    d. *What's changing in this type of job?*
    e. *What kinds of people do well in this type of job?*
    f. *What kinds of people don't seem to like it?*
    g. *What didn't you know before you got into this line of work that you wish someone had told you?*
5. Practice asking these questions with other family members and get their advice on ways to show you have prepared for the interview and how to probe without prying

Debriefing

The Holland Self-Directed Search questionnaire and Informational Interviews are two key activities for exploring career options. But there are many others, of course. However, these are two very effective and oft used ways to get started discussing this very important topic.

No questionnaire can fully assess family members' motivation or drive when exploring career interests. They can only assess general aptitude and interests. Likewise, informational interviews reflect only the perspective of a few people and may not capture what related jobs are like or how the field may change in the future as technology evolves. While imprecise, they are still two of the best available tools today in exploring career options.

Debriefing these two activities happens best when parents and children focus more on a range of career possibilities and less on a particular job. Here's some questions to consider when debriefing any career assessment exercise:

- What did you learn that surprised you?
- What results seem consistent with other assessments or interviews?
- What seemed off base or inconsistent with previous results/interviews?
- What do you want to research or check out further?
- Where else can you go to learn more about this type of job/career and whether it's a good match with your interests/abilities?

Generalizing

Sometimes talking about careers and personal interests can seem like reading a fortune cookie: it all sounds good, and anything is possible. However, the more general or unfocused family members are about career options, the less prepared they will be to pursue a career choice. They don't need to be definitive but spending time on this most important aspect of growing up can be enormously useful.

There are two important aspects of career explorations:

1. *Testing the waters* on interests and abilities.
2. *Finding out* about jobs/careers that are a good match with them.

For teens, in particular, it's important that they keep an open mind and investigate a wide range of career possibilities. Who knows how jobs will change and what might be available for them? Having said that, future jobs will certainly still fit into Holland's six categories and so it can be used with confidence.

These family discussions on career possibilities can lead to related topics such as personal values, educational requirements, and individual motivation. Such purposeful and intentional discussions promote family togetherness and support. Such discussions are certainly not an endpoint—not the finish line—but the starting point for personal understanding. Here's some questions to use to "dive deeper" together while exploring each family member's vocational interests:

- What skills or activities come naturally for me?
- What activities make me happy or energized?
- Who have I talked to that has influenced me most?
- Based on my interests/skills, where should I concentrate my efforts?
- If I were guaranteed career success, what would I do?

Applying

There's an interesting title to a book on teens and careers called *Want a Job? Get Experience. Want Experience? Get a Job.*[3] It can be difficult to get the experience needed to determine if a career is a good fit. Getting related experience helps a lot. It may take some creativity to find ways to "test out" or determine if a certain career is a good fit for you, but it is worth the effort.

It's one thing to *talk* about careers and jobs, it's quite another to *do* something related to it. Consequently, once family members have an idea of the type of jobs or careers they might like that match up with their interests and abilities, help them check out various jobs in that field.

There's a variety of ways to experience what it might be like to work in a specified field or job—even as a teen with no experience. Here's some options:

- *Job shadowing*: Follow someone for a day or a week to see what they do; perform small tasks to get a feel for day-to-day work requirements.
- *Volunteer:* Ask a local company or organization and participate on a project team or help plan an event.
- *Intern:* Paid or unpaid opportunities to work alongside others are often available just for the asking; while interns typically perform less skilled tasks, it is also a way to learn more about that type of work.

3. Don Berliner, *Want a Job? Get Some Experience. Want Experience? Get a Job* (New York: Amacom, 1978).

- *Attend a Career Fair*: While career fairs can be a great source of information, they can also help family members make contacts for job shadowing, internships, and the like.
- *Complementary Work*: There can often be related jobs that can indirectly provide similar work experiences such as CNAs in healthcare or Call Center reps in business or Tech Assistants in many different fields.

SUMMARY

The best way to get good career advice is to ask as many people as possible about what they do. Some of this advice will be helpful, some of it won't be. Try to ask as many "what" and "how" questions as possible. The more that you can help people give *descriptive* replies, the better. Then, you are in a better position to evaluate and compare answers without relying on the evaluation of others.

Besides, people will typically paint a rosy picture of what they do. After all, they chose this career! So, probing and comparing descriptive responses from as many people as possible will lead to a clearer picture of a potential future career.

Importantly, while jobs and careers may change over time, foundational skills will not. Practice being a good problem-solver, team member, adviser, learner, and colleague. Practice these together at home and with your family. There's no better place or way to explore interests or career options than together as a family.

#27

Making Church a Welcoming Place

According to the most recent National Study of Youth and Religion, while young people are increasingly interested in gaining more spirituality, they are also saying they are not finding it in organized religion.[1] Sadly, more young people than in the past are choosing to leave the restored Church as well.

An interesting initiative at BYU-I by Professors Sarah and Eric d'Evegnee has focused on understanding and addressing this trend. They have found that many young people have difficulty dealing with uncertainty and ambiguity both in their daily lives and in understanding historical events in the past. Their website www.faithisnotblind.org has some valuable information including videos and podcasts that will both educate and inspire those dealing with such questions.

In addition to addressing ambiguity and uncertainty, feeling like they belong in the Church and seeing the relevance of the restored gospel in their everyday lives are also common issues among today's youth. Many may feel there could be a larger purpose in life, but don't quite find it in church attendance. They think "they've *heard* it all before;" which, perhaps, they have. But they may also never have *felt* the influence of the Spirit or felt it so long ago that they have forgotten how it feels.

In helping those on the outside looking in, Elder Dallin H. Oaks has suggested that sometimes our approach needs realignment. He suggests that

1. KellieAnn Halvorsen, "BYU-Idaho professors Eric and Sarah d'Evegnée on faith, testimony and reconversion," *Church News Podcast*, 16 Nov. 2021, omny.fm/shows/church-news-podcast/byu-idaho-professors-eric-and-sarah-d-evegn-on-fai.

we can better reframe what we say and do if we consider their timing, not just our own; and recognize that their unexpressed interest in the "fruits of the gospel" may be a better topic than any doctrinal messages. In his October 2016 General Conference address "Sharing the Restored Gospel," he said:

> We need to remember "that people learn when they're ready to learn, not when we're ready to teach them." What *we* are interested in, like the important additional doctrinal teachings in the restored Church, usually isn't what *others* are interested in. Others typically want the *results* of the doctrine, not the doctrine. As they observe or experience the effects of the restored gospel of Jesus Christ in our lives, they feel the Spirit and begin to be interested in the doctrine. They may also be interested when they are seeking more happiness, closeness to God, or a better understanding of the purpose of life. Therefore, we must carefully and prayerfully seek discernment on how to inquire about others' interest to learn more.

The fruits of the gospel, Elder Oaks notes, includes the health code embedded in the Word of Wisdom, the compassion and concern for others inherent in both tithing and the Welfare plan, and the sense of community and belonging that can be found in families and wards. Creating this sense of togetherness in families and wards is an aspiration worth striving for daily among all members.

THE ELEMENT OF SURPRISE

In every good story, in every joke or conversation, in every game or adventure, there is an element of surprise. It's what draws us in, engages us, makes things interesting. It's what keeps us listening or reading or going to the end.

Wards and branches that are inviting and welcoming adopt this "element of surprise" in ordinary ways.

- They get *personal*, in ministering and in get-togethers.
- They *celebrate* holidays, events, and each other's small victories.
- They *connect* emotionally—in class discussions, in the hallways, in texts, in the neighborhood.
- They *give others the floor* who feel isolated.
- They *share spiritual experiences* and invite sharing from others.
- They like *being part of something bigger* than themselves.

In a home-centered Church-supported environment, families and wards learn how to support each other in gospel learning, ministering, and participating in sacred ordinances, according to Elder Quentin L. Cook who introduced this adjustment in General Conference in October 2018. Families and wards have enormous flexibility in how they accomplish these eternal, life-saving goals.

ACTIVITY: A Delightful Sabbath

Accompanying the change to a reduced meeting schedule for home-centered Church-supported Sundays was an increased emphasis on making the Sabbath distinctive, unique, different—a delight.

Think of a time when you felt particularly included in a group or organization outside of your ward or branch.

- What did others say or do to include you?
- What helped you to feel special, that you belonged, and were meant to be there?
- What did you do to become a recognized member of that group?
- What helped you want to stay—even when you weren't sure that you wanted to do so?
- What did you do to let others know you were there "for the long haul"?

Now, think about other people at your ward or branch and what helps you feel that you belong—and that others do as well:

- What do ward or branch members do that increases your sense of belonging?
- Who takes the time to notice you and ask about you?
- What do you do to show others you are accepting and committed to their best interests?
- What scriptures most remind you that you belong to Heavenly Father and His "household of faith"?
- When did you last feel the *companionship of the Holy* Ghost and shared how that felt with others?

DEBRIEFING

There is evidence to suggest that a "sense of belonging" is created when people feel like they are *understood* and *loved*. No single activity can create this sense of belonging, but every meaningful interaction can add to it or reinforce it.

Sister Virginia Pearce, First Counselor in the Young Women General Presidency, speaking at General Conference cited a stanza from a poem by Robert Frost and compared it to "ward families."

> Home is a place where, when you have to go there,
> They have to take you in.
> I should somehow call it
> Something you somehow haven't to deserve.

Wards and branches, Sister Pearce noted, are also places we can go without needing to *deserve* to be there.[2] As children of an Eternal God, we can always go home. But how do we convey that to other family members, especially when someone in a position of authority has said something unkind or a child's classmates seem to shun rather than welcome them?

While painful, problems in a family or ward can unify members. There is nothing quite like working together on a cause, a problem, or an issue that can bridge the gap between righteous aspirations and Christlike living.

Family councils can help. Just as talking together and taking action to promote unity helps a family grow closer. Likewise, discussing and taking action together promotes unity and helps a "ward family" grow closer together.

Here's some topics to discuss in family council to promote belonging at Church:

- How can we "linger longer" after church meetings with those who might feel left out?
- Who can we invite over on Sunday to play Sabbath-appropriate games?
- Who can we emulate that uses social media to promote acceptance and caring?
- How can we "be the change" that we want to see in our ward?

Generalizing

Everyone gets offended at one time or another at church. It's inevitable. It's part of the human condition. As the apostle James notes, "For in many things we offend all" (James 3:2).

Because we rub shoulders together so often in such close quarters, we can see the best and sometimes the worst in each other. How we *interpret*

2. Virginia H. Pearce, "Ward and Branch Families: Part of Heavenly Father's Plan for Us," *Ensign*, Nov. 1993, 79.

unintended (or perhaps even intended) slights determines whether we will take offense or see such things as the natural consequence of ordinary people who simply do very ordinary things.

"A thing, an event, or an expression may be offensive, but you and I can choose not to be offended," Elder David A. Bednar of the Quorum of the Twelve has noted.[3] In other words, we can simply overlook slights, comments, or rebuffs without taking offense at them. Or interpreting them as "I don't belong here."

There is an old saying that suggests "what you think about me is none of my business." This idea is that others' opinions don't define who we are nor our belief in ourselves.

We can *choose* to belong regardless of the circumstances. It starts by not overgeneralizing a single act (or even more) as exclusionary—as a reason not to belong—whether because of our own shortcomings or others' spiritual immaturity. When we define ourselves as children of God and eternally part of His family, we will always belong.

In choosing to belong, we surround ourselves with like-minded others. With such support, we are more resilient, able to cope better with life's stresses, and have an outlet valve for dealing with life's difficulties. Membership gives us meaning.

How can we choose to belong and minimize the occasional sense that we don't "really" belong? Here's some suggestions:

- *Make an effort*: The more we try anything, the easier it becomes. By defining ourselves as "insiders" rather than "outsiders," we are more likely to feel part of things.
- *Practice acceptance:* Take the time to get to know others personally. Make small talk and use it to gradually share more about your background and interests. The more we find out details about others, the more likely we are to see past any differences.
- *Emphasize individuality*: Just as the Savior focused on individuals and avoided putting all Samaritans in the same category, we can do the same.

Applying

Outsiders can be cynical, negative, and scornful. In Lehi's vision of the Tree of Life, those in the large and spurious building are laughing and pointing

3. David A. Bednar, "And Nothing Shall Offend Them," *Ensign,* Nov. 2006, 91.

their fingers, apparently reveling in being *outsiders*. While this "outsiders' syndrome" occurs in other organizations besides the Church, it is perhaps most noticeable in a lay church with very ordinary people.

Infected with the "outsiders' syndrome," such people often can't just let things go, but instead feel obligated to point out various members' flaws. As we read in Proverbs, "A brother offended is harder to be won than a strong city: and their contentions are like the bars of a castle" (Proverbs 18:19).

We may not always be able to persuade others to "come inside," but we can choose to be insiders ourselves. It just takes practice. Sometimes thinking about differences between people or places helps us see what barriers there might be to inviting others inside and how we might be able to do it better ourselves. Here's some ideas for doing that.

- If you won free lessons for a dance style that's completely unfamiliar to you, how would you feel?
- When at school or work have others spoken in a language you didn't understand? Did you think they were talking about you?
- If you grew up in a foreign country, what would seem weird about where you live now?

The more we practice being *insiders*, the more natural it becomes.

SUMMARY

Creating a sense of belonging at church is about enabling others to become "insiders." Recognizing this may be easier for some—especially extroverts—than for others whose natural tendency may be toward introversion.

While extroverts may find it easier to meet new people and become accessible to those who are uncertain, introverts have a harder time extending themselves to others. While we each have our own innate tendencies, we can learn to become more open and accessible to others.

In *The Secret Life of Introverts,* Jenn Granneman emphasizes that embracing her own tendency to hang back and let others take charge helped her reshape her life. Acknowledging that she was an introvert gave her a way to identify her own tendencies without using them to justify remaining aloof or feeling awkward around others. Instead, she adopted strategies that helped her stretch her comfort zone and expand her world view.

This perspective on introverts also applies to those who feel like outsiders. Here's some tips she gives that apply equally to introverts and those who want to encourage them to join in and "belong" as insiders:

- Ask questions, find common ground when meeting or talking to others.
- Be willing to be vulnerable and share missteps or uncertainties. Give up the myth of perfection—no one has it, no one needs it.
- Give yourself an "invitation" to learn more about others.
- Make a comment in class—especially if it shows your efforts to do something which did not go particularly well. Others will typically rally around your sincere efforts.
- Send a text each Sunday to tell someone—specifically—what you liked about their talk or comment in class. Such texts may be easier to send than a face-to-face comment yet help establish a connection with others. [4]

4. Jenn Granneman, *The Secret Lives of Introverts: Inside Our Hidden World* (Skyhorse Publishing, 2017).

#28

Teaming Up with Teachers

IT CAN SEEM TO SOME THAT HOME AND CHURCH ARE TWO DIFFERENT places and "never the twain shall meet." But in an ideal home-centered Church-supported environment, they overlap and should be aligned with each other.

When parents and teachers at church are on the same page, they can do more than discuss classroom behavior. They can reinforce key messages without simply becoming redundant. Brother Jan E. Newman, Second Counselor in the Sunday School General Presidency, in his October 2021 General Conference address "Teaching in the Savior's Way," invited "leaders and teachers in every organization of the Church to counsel together with parents and youth in order to dramatically improve teaching at every level— in stakes, in wards, and in homes."

Teacher council meetings provide a unique opportunity for parents and teachers to *counsel together* in personal and intentional ways. Just as cars have regular tune ups, so teachers can have regular discussions with parents to get their input on topics and methods that appeal most to their children. While this kind of input and feedback may not have happened much in the past, teacher councils provide a new opportunity for it to happen regularly.

There's lot of different ways parents and teachers can team up in sharing their thoughts and suggestions with each other. While either parents or teachers can initiate such a discussion, here's some tips for teachers:

- Send a text with something a family member shared in class and ask for more details.

- Linger in the hallway and ask parents about their child's favorite scripture stories.
- Visit in a family's home and share a handout that reinforces a class discussion.

Parents can do similar things, as well as share with teachers their family members' interests, hobbies, and goals. This could include telling teachers about school projects or books each family member is reading. The more parents can let teachers become partners with them, the better gospel instruction and learning will occur.

Activity: Partnership with Teachers

Teachers are not accustomed to hearing from parents unless there is some kind of problem. In addition, while *Come, Follow Me* makes it easy for parents to know the *content* of Sunday School and Primary classes, without some coordination there could be a lot of *duplication* and unnecessary repetition rather than helpful reinforcement.

Flip the script by asking teachers to connect regularly with you about your children in their classes and topics they plan to present from *Come, Follow Me.* Then, use this as input for building on each other's approach. Make this an ongoing interaction, not just a one-time discussion.

Opening a dialogue with teachers doesn't require a formal meeting. A phone call or text exchange or even a brief discussion at the end of the regular church meeting block can all be good ways to get started. Here's some ways to help make this process work:

- *Overcome inertia*: Getting started is always the hardest part because parent/teacher discussions are unexpected unless there's a classroom behavior problem.
- *Prime the pump*: Let teachers know that you want to create a partnership and that you'd like to get support for family goals.
- *Share stories:* Tell teachers when your child remembered a lesson or experience from class; use these examples to show how your child learns best.
- *Share ideas:* Tell teachers prior to Sunday meetings what you've discussed in *Come, Follow Me* so they will be able to build on your family's discussion and interaction.

- *Ask for ideas*: Many times, teachers may not have time to use all of the material they have prepared. Ask them to send you material they may not have used so that you can use it in your family discussion.
- *Strengthen each other*: This interaction is an opportunity for parents and teachers to help and support each other; make it a mutual learning opportunity.

Debriefing

When parents explore what they have gleaned from each teacher interaction, they are collaborating in a meaningful way. While partnerships don't have to be difficult, they require some effort to create and maintain. As parents, you likely already have very different relationships with each of your children's teachers. Build on whatever relationship you have to enhance the learning experience for your children in each teacher's class.

By using this approach, parents are inviting teachers to become consultants to their family. While informal, it allows teachers to minister and align with family goals. It makes them partners.

Family Councils and Teacher Councils can both benefit from members sharing their experience in building this kind of family and teacher partnership. It allows families and teachers to take a broader look at their role by sharing in family goals and not simply becoming dispensers of information on Sundays.

Like any partnership, it can become stronger if it is assessed regularly. Here's some questions to assist with assessing such partnerships:

- How can we avoid becoming defensive and stay open with each other?
- How can we create and nourish a trusting relationship between us?
- How do we ensure confidentiality on anything personal?
- How do we inspire and support each other?
- How do we promote a community of learners among us?

Generalizing

No one succeeds in a silo. We need each other. That's why we are part of a ward, a quorum, a class, or any other group. Today's stranger may be tomorrow's teacher-partner.

Partnerships thrive on open communication and shared goals. They also depend on alignment among the principals involved in the partnership: whether personal, business, or community.

Good partnerships "begin with the end in mind;" a popular concept in Steven Covey's book *7 Habits of Highly Successful People.* In gospel partnerships, it means seeing each other not only as children of God but also as celestial beings filled with love and light. It means working backwards from this goal to consider activities and insights that would be helpful in achieving it.

Applying

Alma asked that we consider what it would be like to be in God's presence—really project ourselves into the future and stand right along beside Him—and then work backwards to the present day.

> Do ye exercise faith in the redemption of him who created you? Do you look forward with an eye of faith, and view this mortal body raised in immortality, and this corruption raised in incorruption, to stand before God to be judged according to the deeds which have been done in the mortal body?
>
> I say unto you, can you imagine to yourselves that ye hear the voice of the Lord, saying unto you, in that day: Come unto me ye blessed, for behold, your works have been the works of righteousness upon the face of the earth? (Alma 5:15–16)

SUMMARY

Purposely and intentionally developing partnerships between parents and Church teachers may seem easy, but rarely occurs. Unless there is a "behavior problem," historically parents and Church teachers rarely talk about common gospel learning or family goals.

Come, Follow Me changes that. It makes it easier to overcome the "passive logjam" that typically occurs in Church teaching assignments by expecting parents and teachers to reinforce curriculum goals without duplicating information. It's one thing to reinforce each other at home and at church, it's quite another to read the same scriptures, recite the same stories, and ask the same questions.

Discussing common goals together may seem awkward at first for parents as well as teachers. But overcoming a tendency simply to let things drift can produce remarkable benefits both for teachers and family members.

Families and teachers can become better aligned, more willing to share insights and experiences, and better able to nurture and inspire.

If teachers are aware of family and personal goals for family members, the common *Come, Follow Me* curriculum can be used not only for alignment but also to avoid the kind of repetition that causes kids to check out.

And it doesn't take much. Depending on the relationship that parents may already have with various teachers, an occasional text, a discussion in the hallway, or a personal visit may be useful in sharing family goals and discussing ways teachers can reinforce them in the classroom. Teachers can also share areas in a lesson they plan to emphasize so that parents can build on what a teacher may focus on during a particular lesson.

#29

Refrain from Being Quick to Judge

All families are emotionally complex. After living with each other for years, family members are especially adept at *pushing each other's buttons:* those emotional triggers that needle us sometimes just to see our reaction. It happens for lots of different reasons: some good—to challenge and inspire us—and others not so good—to control or diminish us. While families vary, the emotional baggage that families accumulate is undeniable. Often, we simultaneously rely on and resist advice from family members who can be either too close for comfort or too far away to share what's really going on.

We become judgmental when feeling *wronged, superior, or angry.* When this happens, we tend to:

- See others worst traits or actions
- Blame them for their misfortunes
- Justify our criticism of them

These same dynamics are at work in nuclear families, extended families, and the human family. Understanding they are part of the mortal condition—"the natural man"—helps us resist its influence. When we better recognize where being *judgmental* comes from, we are more likely to help family members overcome its negative influence.

King Mosiah famously decried being judgmental of the poor in the Book of Mormon but what he had to say applies to any situation where we are *quick to judge* others:

> For behold, are we not all beggars? Do we not all depend upon the same Being, even God, for all the substance which we have, for

> both food and raiment, and for gold, and for silver, and for all the riches which we have of every kind?
>
> And behold, even at this time, ye have been calling on his name, and begging for a remission of your sins. And has he suffered that ye have begged in vain? Nay; he has poured out his Spirit upon you, and has caused that your hearts should be filled with joy, and has caused that your mouths should be stopped that ye could not find utterance, so exceedingly great was your joy.
>
> And now, if God, who has created you, on whom you are dependent for your lives and for all that ye have and are, doth grant unto you whatsoever ye ask that is right, in faith, believing that ye shall receive, O then, how ye ought to impart of the substance that ye have one to another. (Mosiah 4:19–21)

Elder Jeffrey R. Holland summarized and suggested how these verses might apply in our own day and in our individual circumstances:

> Don't we all cry out for help and hope and answers to prayers? Don't we all beg for forgiveness for mistakes we have made and troubles we have caused? Don't we all implore that grace will compensate for our weaknesses, that mercy will triumph over justice at least in our case? Little wonder that King Benjamin says we *obtain* a remission of our sins by pleading to God, who compassionately responds, but we *retain* a remission of our sins by compassionately responding to the poor who plead to us.[1]

While Elder Holland is talking about reaching out to the poor, poverty exists in ways that have nothing to do with money. Poverty occurs when we don't have enough food, shelter, friends, or advocates.

When people with disabilities are excluded because of their limitations, it is an especially debilitating kind of poverty. Such was the case for Helen Keller who was excluded from most family activities as a child because of her disabilities. Only with the help of her extraordinary teacher and mentor Annie Sullivan was Helen able to learn and eventually become accepted by her family and later society in general.

Helen Keller wrote in her autobiography that people often felt uncomfortable around her, as if her disability somehow diminished them. At age 14 she became friends with Mark Twain, and they stayed friends for the rest of Twain's life. She wrote of him:

1. Jeffrey R. Holland, "Are We Not All Beggars," *Ensign,* Nov. 2014, 41.

> He treated me not as a freak, but as a handicapped woman seeking a way to circumvent extraordinary difficulties.[2]

Rather than feeling sorry for her, Twain and others overcame their own feelings of awkwardness and embraced her differences just as she embraced theirs.

Activity: Experiencing Disabilities

In a 2014 survey, 67% of respondents said they felt uncomfortable around people with disabilities. Among those who reported feeling uncomfortable, half said they would not want to work with anyone who was either deaf or blind.[3]

Perhaps there is no better way to reduce possible anxieties about disabilities than to experience them. This activity can easily be done at home for whatever length of time the family may be able to devote to it. However, the longer the time spent (several hours at least), the better. Here's how it works:

Tell family members that today they will all experience some kind of disability. Ask them to do as many things as they normally would do, but they can ask for help when needed.

Blindfold some family members, put headphones with "white background noise" on others. Place others in a borrowed wheelchair. Put heavy socks on the hands of others.

Give each family member a list of tasks to complete such as tying their shoes, putting a puzzle together, sewing on a button, building a tower with only drinking straws and masking tape, writing a letter, eating spaghetti, getting small items from another room, playing a board game, and the like.

After 30–60 minutes, switch circumstances for each family member so they experience a different kind of disability.

Debriefing

Talking about this activity is where the real benefits occur. Visit together as a family and consider these questions:

---

2. Hadley Meares, "Helen Keller and Mark Twain Had an Unlikely Friendship That Spanned More Than a Decade," *Biography*, 1 Jun. 2020, https://www.biography.com/news/helen-keller-mark-twain-friendship.

3. "How to Stop Being Awkward with Individuals Who Have Disabilities Right Now," Hand in Hand, www.handinhandqc.org/blog, accessed Jan. 2023.

- How did it feel not to be able to do some things?
- What did you find most difficult to do?
- Did you ever get frustrated or feel irritable?
- What helped you cope best?
- What did others do that helped you?
- What did others do that you didn't like or that seemed to emphasize your limitations?
- What did you learn from this activity?

Generalizing

Family members can reflect on this experience, including how differences can cause us to feel awkward at first, but with shared experiences such discomfort diminishes. This occurs not only with disabilities but with cultural, ethnic, religious, and other differences as well. There is nothing like a shared experience to see people or cultures or circumstances differently, in a new light, and with a better understanding. Here's an additional discovery-learning activity about not being quick to judge but instead recognizing individual differences.

1. Give each family member a potato from a bag.
2. Ask them each to describe their potato with as much detail as possible.
3. Put the potatoes back in a bag and ask:
    a. *Before being given a potato, would you have thought "all potatoes are just the same"?*
    b. *How did describing a potato to the family change how you looked at your potato?*
4. Roll the potatoes out of the bag and ask family members to find their potato. Ask them how they were able to pick out their own potato.
5. Ask family members if they tend to lump people in a group—maybe even *label* them as all the same—and not see their individual differences. Some groups might include:
    - Band members
    - Cheerleaders
    - Kids who live in the city
    - Kids who live in the country
    - Kids who live in a certain part of town
    - All girls
    - All boys

6. Ask family members about the benefits and limitations of such labels. Here's some examples to help get started with a discussion:
    a. *Advantages: Helps reduce ambiguity, provides convenient ways to discuss common characteristics, helps provide focus and pay attention.*
    b. *Disadvantages: Obscures individual differences, promotes stereotypes, creates barriers, can lead to "us" versus "them" thinking and actions such as blaming and regarding others with suspicion.*

Applying

Families can not only learn more about community differences but can have shared experiences with people from other backgrounds by doing the following:

- Attend a service or holiday celebration by another religious group.
- Visit a homeless shelter and assist during a meal or unexpected weather conditions.
- Go to a senior center and assist with a craft or game.
- Volunteer to teach a lesson at an English as Second Language class.
- Make holiday greeting cards and take them to neighbors or assisted living centers.

Following these visits, it can be helpful to discuss what family members experienced and learned.

- How did you feel when you first arrived: Curious? Uncertain? More advanced? Out of place?
- What helped you feel more comfortable?
- Who did you talk to that made an impression on you?
- How do you see people you meet differently?
- How do you see our family differently?
- What could we do if/when we visit again?

SUMMARY

In his book *The Pause Principle*, Kevin Cashman describes ways that we sabotage ourselves with hasty and impulsive decisions.[4] There's an old saying

4. Kevin Cashman, *The Pause Principle: Step Back to Lead Forward* (Berrett-Koehler Publishers, 2012).

that many times it is necessary to "slow down in order to go fast." Pushing the "pause" button can help us gather more facts, avoid making snap judgments based on initial impressions, and find out more about other people and situations before rushing to judgment. Here's three additional ways to help do that:

- *Consult others:* Ask trusted friends for advice who may be able to supplement your own perspective.
- *Distract yourself:* Reckoning a tendency toward hasty judgments can be blunted by taking a walk, listening to music, or even playing a game. All of these give yourself space to consider alternatives and become more intentional about next steps.
- *Ask yourself:* What would your father/best friend/neighbor or other significant person in your life do to learn more about a certain topic? This can help you see things from a different perspective and add to your own thinking on the matter.

#30

Staying Curious

We can all get bogged down in day-to-day activities and overlook the wonders around us. Children are naturally curious and want to know as much as they can about the world in which we live. From looking at the night sky to finding out about other people and cultures, exploring things that are new and different enhance this curiosity.

There is a concept called "intellectual humility" that is being studied by researchers at Duke and Fordham Universities as a fundamental building block in the learning process. More than the opposite of "close mindedness," it focuses on people's ability to see awe and become curious about the wider world.

There are many obstacles to staying curious especially as children get older. Because there are so many divergent points of view today, knowing *who to believe* can alternatively make family members uncomfortable exploring new ideas or even considering them at all. Fear and self-centeredness—*a know-it-all attitude*—destroys curiosity.

Curiosity is all about a willingness to suspend judgment while exploring new facts or new ideas about us, others, and our place in the universe. It is remarkable to me that after teaching seminary or institute during the past seven years how unwilling teens seem to be to explore new ideas about themselves or their world. Their minds are made up about so many things! There's certainly much to be said about drawing on previously experiences and relying on faithful advice in charting the future. Perhaps there is also room for being vulnerable and questioning some assumptions about things we may have learned and our views about others. Becoming vulnerable in fact may be the key to developing lasting relationships with others.[1]

National survey data in the United States shows that curiosity declines dramatically from early middle school through high school. Kids get caught up in grades and performing well rather than being curious and making new discoveries. Dr. Angela Duckworth, founder of Character Labs, offers this very practical suggestion to reverse this trend:

> One practical idea is for kids of any age to spend at least five minutes every day asking questions and exploring their curiosity, even if it doesn't lead to their SAT score being higher or some chore being done. Just asking the questions that naturally come to mind.[2]

This next activity helps promote such questions and lets family members daydream a little about themselves and their world.

ACTIVITY: Intriguing Questions card game

In this activity, family members not only respond to each question, but also reward each other for their answers. The game is about responding thoughtfully and creatively as well as about the benefits and limitations of rewards.

1. Write each *Intriguing Question* on an index card.
2. Have family members explain their answer to each question by giving their most creative response.
3. Shuffle the cards after each turn so they are thoroughly mixed up.
4. After each person's response, family members rate their reply based on how creative and thoughtful their answer is.
5. Use a limited number of different colored poker chips. Give each family member 3 times as many white chips as red chips and twice as many blue chips as red chips. Tell them the value of each chip is as follows:

    Red: 5
    Blue: 3
    White: 1

1. Brené Brown, *The Power of Vulnerability: Teachings of Authenticity, Connection, and Courage* (Sounds True, 2013), audiobook.
2. Pontz, Eden. 2021. "Gratitude, Curiosity, and Building Character in Teens." Center for Parent and Teen Communication, August. https://parentandteen.com/qa-duckworth-gratitude-curiosity/.

Play several rounds. After the final round, debrief the game together. Debriefing is part of the game. Do not overlook it.

Intriguing Questions

What have you always wanted to buy/get?
What's the weirdest dream you've ever had?
Who do you most admire outside the Church or our family?
What historical event would you most like to have witnessed?
What questions do you hate to answer?
What are some ridiculous goals you have in life?
What's the meanest thing you've ever seen someone do?
What is the most spontaneous and funny thing you've ever done?
What personality trait do you wish you had?
What's something that you think most people learn too late?
If you had a million dollars that you had to give away, what would you do?
Who is the most impressive person alive today outside the Church?
If you could go to just one place/time as a time traveler, where would you go?
What event in your life might make a good movie?
What does a perfect day for you look like?
What is the nicest thing someone has said about you that was unexpected?
What do you value most in a friend?
What are the three most valuable things you learned from your mom?
What are the three most valuable things you learned from your dad?
What recurring nighttime dreams do you have?
What surprises you when you look into the night sky?
What's the most impressive thing you've seen in nature?
When you stare at a tree, what do you notice?
What bird, bug, or animal in nature intrigues you most?
What part of God's creations seems most unusual to you?

Debriefing

Children learn to follow (or resist) following rules as they grow and mature. But neither following nor resisting rules promotes curiosity. It's something different altogether. It's about imagining and investigating, seeking and experimenting, trying new things and valuing new experiences. It's about seeing wonder and awe in the world around us.

Research shows that seeing *awe* actually helps us become healthier and happier. We see the world around us as a place where we can learn rather than worry about, a place beyond man-made monuments to see God in all His majesty, "who is in the bosom of eternity, who is in the midst of all things" (D&C 88:13).

In debriefing this family activity, consider some or all of these questions:

- What three "Intriguing Questions" did you like answering the best?
- What 2–3 "Intriguing Questions" made you the most uncomfortable?
- Alma said, "all things denote there is a God; yea, even the earth. and all things that are upon the face of it, yea, and its motion, yea, and also all the planets which move in their regular form do witness there is a Supreme Creator" (Alma 30:44). What natural wonders would you like to know more about?

Generalizing

Curiosity is about asking questions and letting kids find answers for themselves. Too often parents can become too quick to give kids answers to their questions rather than encouraging them to find answers for themselves. Sure, a little guidance helps. But rather than give answers, try to stimulate curiosity with your responses. Here's some suggestions:

- What do you think?
- What have you thought about already?
- If you wanted to know more about that, where could you look?
- There could be different points of view about that. How can you sort through those differences to get a better answer?

Applying

The scriptures and the words of the living prophets provide practical answers to many of life's perplexing questions. Encourage family members to "feast upon the word of God" (2 Nephi 31:20) and encourage them with all of their learning to get understanding. (Proverbs 4:7).

There is so much information on the internet on many subjects that it can be overwhelming. Learning how to "fact check" the internet can be pivotal to get the real story. Teens can do this by using only reliable sources and asking others for help when trying to determine the veracity of a story. Help family members "seek learning, even by study and also by faith" (D&C 88:118) as a first resort, not an afterthought.

- Use the topical guide in the scriptures or the Gospel app as a starting place when family members curiosity is sparked on a topic.
- Refer to general conference talks and gospel essays on relevant topics.
- Identify faithful subject matter experts for family members to visit with via social media or email.

SUMMARY

Albert Einstein once said, "The important thing is not to stop questioning. . . . Never lose a holy curiosity."[3] Asking questions takes effort. It is not a passive activity. And it is this proactive stance that builds kids self-reliance and self-confidence. They can inquire and discover for themselves. There is perhaps nothing so fundamental to the gospel of Jesus Christ than asking, seeking, and finding answers to our questions directly from the Holy Ghost. It was Joseph Smith's curiosity about which church to join that caused him to go to the Sacred Grove to find answers. It is a divine pattern for all of us to emulate.

3. Albert Einstein, "Old Man's Advice to Youth: 'Never Lose a Holy Curiosity,'" *LIFE Magazine,* 2 May 1955, 64.

Chapter 6

Teaching and Parenting—Creating Home-Centered Learning Environments

Parenting styles vary and there is "no one right way" to parent. After a massive study spanning more than 50 years and hundreds of families, psychologist David McClelland at Harvard University concluded that no single technique or approach could be ascribed to successful families who were both emotionally resilient and achievement oriented. However, McClelland and others found that two critical elements seemed to characterize successful families:

1. Parents genuinely enjoyed being with their children. While they did lots of activities together—which varied widely across families and changed over time—there was a real sense of togetherness fostered by simply enjoying each other's company.
2. Fathers, in particular, were present "in the moment." They were proactively involved in leading family discussions, helping with homework, offering tips on social interaction, and providing support for daily living. Mothers, they noted, did this more frequently so when fathers were engaged it was more noticeable.

From this research, McClelland emphasized the important role of teaching children through shared experiences, which families then reflected on during holidays and reunions. It is not simply doing things together that matter, he noted, but doing them and then discussing what it meant to the family. This kind of guided discussion makes all the difference in developing character, competence, and creating strong family connections.[1]

In Doctrine and Covenants 105:10, the Lord tells the Prophet Joseph about the important connections between teaching and experience. Speaking to members of the "churches abroad," the Lord said:

> That they themselves may be prepared, and that my people may be taught more perfectly, and have experience, and know more perfectly concerning their duty, and the things which I require at their hands.

We learn by doing when we take the time to process our life experiences with others. Children—regardless of their age—are particularly adept at learning from experience when shown how to debrief, generalize, and apply life experiences.

John Dewey, the creator of the Dewey Decimal System and a professor at the University of Chicago, is attributed to saying, "We don't learn from experience, we learn from reflecting on our experience." Without reflecting, examining, and sharing our observations with others, no learning takes place. This is the "how to" in learning from experience. This is what families must create to develop a learning culture in their homes.

Life experiences can be positive and negative. Negative, stressful experiences are not necessarily bad if we learn from them. However, too often, we draw the wrong conclusions from negative experiences, and rather than helping us learn from them, they cause us to be wary, withdrawn, or suspicious. There is an old saying that without thoroughly debriefing lessons learned from experience, then "the only thing we learn from experience is that we don't learn from experience." We must be deliberate in observing, assessing, and confirming life lessons in order to ensure that we learn eternal truths and not inaccurate speculation from our experience.

Learning is far more than repetition or simply picking up a new habit. Real learning has at least three distinct components:

- Ability to observe and accurately "take in" what is happening around us.
- Proficiency in accurately processing new information and discerning when and how to use it.
- Willingness to "get to the bottom of things," to go beyond what someone may tell us to find out things for ourselves.

1. George Valliant, *Adaptation to Life* (NY: Little, Brown, and Co.,1978).

Much is made these days about developing "critical thinking skills."[2] While there are many ways this can be done, encouraging family members to develop and test their own hypothesis is one important feature. The scriptures emphasis this same approach by encouraging us to "experiment upon [Christ's] words" (Alma 32:27) and "prove what is that good, and acceptable, and perfect, will of God" (Romans 12:2) and "prove all things: hold fast that which is good" (1 Thes. 5:21).

In his book *How We Know What Isn't So,* the psychologist Thomas Gilovich suggests "the world does not play fair. Instead of providing us with clear information that would enable us to 'know' better, it presents us with messy data that are random, incomplete, unrepresentative, ambiguous, inconsistent, unpalatable, or secondhand."[3]

Learning is an intentional act. It starts with determining what we may need to learn, using experience to process events, and engaging others to help validate what we have discovered. In many regards, life skills cannot really be *taught* in the standard sense of the term—it's not just a matter of giving or getting new information—but they can easily be *learned* with experience and a little guidance.

HOW FAMILIES CAN DEVELOP A LEARNING CULTURE

Some family cultures are "learning-friendly" while others may be "learning-averse." In *learning-averse* family cultures, there are tons of rules, constant and unrelenting expectations, and continuous reinforcement for following well-defined family plans. The emphasis is on *conformity*, not learning.

By contrast, in "learning-friendly" family cultures, there is a sense of wonder among family members, an emphasis on not taking what is "known" for granted, and a willingness to do the hard work of figuring out how things really work. This learning-friendly culture is shared among family members, not just determined by parents.

Life skills and habits are developed best in the home, we know that. More than simply declaring this known fact, parents must consciously assess and develop these skills with other family members rather than simply expecting they will occur on their own. And, of course, giving lectures or even just reading about them is not only insufficient, but can even work crosswise in their development. Personal growth occurs through discovery,

2. Michael Baker, *The Basics of Critical Thinking* (NY: The Critical Thinking Skills Co, 2015).

3. Thomas Gilovich, *How We Know What Isn't So: The Fallibility of Human Reason in Everyday Life* (Free Press, 1993), 3.

planning, acting, and reflecting as described in the *Children and Youth Guidebook,4* which can be used together with discovery-learning methods described throughout this book.

When family members learn a new skill, such as playing the piano or woodworking or any other tangible or intangible skill, *how* they become proficient can be nurtured so children see the learning process itself as a transferable skill. Beyond recognizing notes on a page and turning them into a melody on a keyboard, parents can help children grasp the innate process of becoming skillful at something through diligence and discovery.

Creating a learning-friendly family culture is the sum of multiple factors sustained through intentionally focusing on the following five factors:

1. *Parents example*: Children see parents learning new habits, skills, and becoming *beginners* in various ways themselves.
2. *Openness to new ways of doing things*: Reinforcement for asking questions, taking appropriate risks, exploring.
3. O*ngoing support for sibling collaboration*: A sense of "we're in this together" prevails in the home.
4. P*urposeful play*: Both formally through games and structured activities and informally through observing and debriefing ordinary events.
5. R*egular discussions*: Quantity is as important as quality in learning by doing; its far more than "one and done" to inculcate new habits into new mindsets.

No doubt we have all heard the saying "You can't teach an old dog new tricks." It's not true. In fact, learning occurs at any age if we are willing to think and act like *beginners*. Learning is a mindset as well as a skill. As Maria reminds us in *The Sound of Music:* "Let's start at the very beginning." It is there that family members become learners together.

HOW TO BECOME A LIFELONG *BEGINNER*

In learning-friendly family environments, everyone is "in it" together. Parents are not on the sidelines scrolling on their phones reading the news or paying household bills. Kids are not the only ones doing something while parents watch and implicitly (or explicitly) judge, coach, or reward them. In discovery learning, everyone is a beginner.

4. *Children and Youth Guidebook: An Introductory Guide for Parents and Leaders* (The Church of Jesus Christ of Latter-day Saints, 2019), churchofjesuschrist.org.

Beginners recognize that their knowledge, skills, and perhaps even aptitudes are limited so they are much more open to giving up what little they know and instead find out about things for "the very first time." Researchers say that children learn a new language better than adults only because they approach it as if it were a "first language" for them, while adults approach learning a new language as if it is a "second language." In other words, kids accept a new language with its inherent individuality while adults are constantly relating back to what they "already know." For kids, such learning is fresh and new. For adults, it is a different process of unlearning and relearning.

Claude Shannon, an MIT mathematician and the father of information theory that launched the digital age in which we now live, was known to try many different pursuits unrelated to his career. He approached each of them—juggling, poetry, electronic designs—as if he knew nothing at all about them. He wanted to eliminate his own filters, his own biases, his own unexamined assumptions. By doing so, he became a beginner in every sense of the word and used what he learned to ignite his curiosity in everything else that he did.[5]

Like other skills, becoming a *beginner* is a learned ability. And like other life skills, it is developed through discovery: assessing, debriefing, generalizing, and applying.

Here's a good place to start, a way of assessing a family's (or a family member's) *beginner's mindset*:

- Are we genuinely committed to learning or is it just a slogan?
- Do we insist on telling others precisely how to do things or are we willing to let them learn on their own?
- Do we encourage *question-asking* or rely mostly on telling?
- Do we actually listen to others in discussions or mostly dismiss them?
- Does debriefing seem like a chore or is it a natural part of how we talk with each other?
- Are we able to express divergent points of view without feeling attacked?
- Do we look for gospel truths as the foundation of what we do and how we think or is it just one among other ways of thinking about the world?

5. David Tse, "How Claude Shannon Invented the Future," *Quanta Magazine,* 22 Dec. 2020, www.quantamagazine.org.

- Are we invested in each other in the family or does everyone do their own thing?
- Can we identify what holds us back when starting something new?
- Do we rely on the Holy Ghost to teach us "all truth"?
- Do we look for new possibilities or simply recite "tried and true" catch phrases?
- Do we identify and test preconceptions we may have about ourselves or others?
- Do we have a sense of playfulness in family discussions or are most things overly serious to us?
- Do we express a sense of gratitude and wonder or are we more likely to see the dark side of things?
- Do we see each other's possibilities more than limitations?
- Are we able to slow down and process events and experiences or is it simply on to the next activity?
- Do we live in a world of "shoulds" or do we strive to "live in the moment"?
- Do we constantly need to be "right" or are we willing to consider other options?
- When faced with a problem or dilemma, do we see many possibilities or only one right way?
- Do we seek to learn, or to show how smart we are?

Elder David A. Bednar in the April 2019 General Conference stressed that our homes are the best places to create such lifelong learning environments.

> We should not expect the Church as an organization to teach or tell us everything we need to know and do to become devoted disciples and endure valiantly to the end. Rather, our personal responsibility is to learn what we should learn, to live as we know we should live, and to become who the Master would have us become. And our homes are the ultimate setting for learning, living and becoming.[6]

CHILDREN'S AND YOUTH GUIDEBOOK

In the priesthood session of the April 2021 General Conference, President Russell M. Nelson invited us to periodically reflect on our experiences and share them with others. Here he uses the COVID-19 pandemic as an

6. David A. Bednar, "Prepared to Obtain Every Needful Thing," *Ensign,* May 2019, 102.

example because of its profound, worldwide impact, but it can be applied to all life experiences:

> My dear brethren, there are many things the Lord wants us to learn from our experiences during this pandemic. I have listed only four. I invite you to make your own list, consider it carefully, and share it with those you love.[7]

In essence, he is asking us to debrief. One of the ways that we can follow through on this request is to use the *Children's* and *Youth Guidebooks* to consider and record what family members have learned from the pandemic as well as other experiences. As President Nelson notes, we learn from experience when we examine what we may have learned, write it down, and share it with others.

The Church's *Personal Development: Youth Guidebook*, as well as the one for children, includes "A Pattern for Growth" that mirrors the discovery learning process described in this book.[8] Here are the steps and some assessment questions from the guidebook:

Discover what you need to work on.

- What do I feel I should learn or change in my life?
- What spiritual habits do I need to develop or improve?

Plan how you will do it.

- Why is this important to me?
- What plans can I make now to overcome challenges I may face?

Act on your plan in faith.

- What has worked? Why?
- What has not worked? Why not?
- What else can I try?
- How can I learn from setbacks?

Reflect on what you have learned.

- How have I grown?
- How can I use what I've learned to serve others?
- How can I continue growing in this area?

7. Russell M. Nelson, "What We Are Learning and Will Never Forget," *Ensign*, May 2021, 80.
8. *Personal Development: Youth Guidebook* (The Church of Jesus Christ of Latter-day Saints, 2019), 7–15, churchofjesuschrist.org.

AN ETERNAL JOURNEY

The purpose of the gospel is to come closer to Christ in what we know, how we think, and what we do. It is a continuous process of conversion, of discovering the "mind and will of the Lord" and applying it in our lives. As the scriptures illustrate, conversion is a process, not an event. It is a process of personal growth and development that leads us, like the Savior, to become like our Heavenly Father in outlook, attributes, and actions.

It is a lifelong journey. It is never ending either for parents or children. It is realizing that we never fully *arrive* but instead are constantly learning, growing, improving. As President Lorenzo Snow said:

> There is a danger of our being satisfied with a superficial advancement, with merely advancing on the surface. We talk of walking in the light of the Spirit and of feeling it upon us, but do we do these things? We ought to dig deep into the things of God, lay our foundation upon the rock, until we come to that water which shall be in us an everlasting fountain of eternal life.[9]

While "dig[ging] deep into the things of God" we not only discover who He is but also who we are. We deepen our conversion. Interestingly, as Elder David A. Bednar pointed out in his October 2020 General Conference address, this learning process is rarely facilitated by actual tests. "Interestingly, however, the word *test* is not found even one time in the scriptural text of the standard works in English. Rather, words such as *prove, examine,* and *try* are used . . .."[10] I find that these words are more about discovery and growth.

Consider these scriptures:

> And we will prove them herewith, to see if they will do all things whatsoever the Lord their God shall command them; (Abraham 3:25)

> Examine me, O Lord, and prove me; try my reins and my heart.
> For thy lovingkindness is before mine eyes: and I have walked in thy truth. (Psalms 26:2–3)

> And be not conformed to this world: but be ye transformed by the renewing of your mind, that ye may prove what is that good, and acceptable, and perfect, will of God. (Romans 12:2)

---

9. Lorenzo Snow, "Lifelong Conversion: Continuing to Advance in the Principles of Truth," *Teachings of Presidents of the Church: Lorenzo Snow* (The Church of Jesus Christ of Latter-day Saints, 2012),66.

10. David A. Bednar, "We Will Prove Them Herewith," *Ensign,* Nov. 2020, 8.

> But let every man prove his own work, and then shall he have rejoicing in himself alone, and not in another. (Galatians 6:4)

> Examine yourselves, whether ye be in the faith; prove your own selves. (2 Corinthians 13:5)

Helping our children—and ourselves—realize that there is no need to prove ourselves to others is vital in maintaining a focus on Jesus Christ. He alone is our advocate, our mediator, and our standard. More champion and healer than judge, He wants us to act in faith, look inward to examine ourselves by gospel standards and look outward in serving others so that our hearts have "great experience[s] of wisdom and knowledge" (Ecclesiastes 1:16).

About the Author

Norman C Hill is an Affiliate Associate Professor at the Ballard Center for Social Impact at Brigham Young University and a Global Fellow with the W.K Kellogg Foundation. He was Vice President Human Resources for the Reliant Energy Delivery Group and a Human Resources manager for ExxonMobil. He served as Mission President for the Ghana Accra West and Sierra Leone Freetown missions and has taught Seminary or Institute in Texas, Louisiana, and Utah. He is the author of seven previous books and more than two dozen articles in the Ensign, Liahona New Era, and LDS Living. His wife Raelene passed away in 2015 and he married Stephanie in 2017. Together, they have 8 children and 37 grandchildren in their "bonus family."